To Jane

With Lov...

Ken x

# PEP
# Talk

# PEP
# Talk

Positivity • Empowerment • Performance

## KEN HANCOTT

The Book Guild Ltd

First published in Great Britain in 2020 by
The Book Guild Ltd
9 Priory Business Park
Wistow Road, Kibworth
Leicestershire, LE8 0RX
Freephone: 0800 999 2982
www.bookguild.co.uk
Email: info@bookguild.co.uk
Twitter: @bookguild

Typeset in 12pt Minion Pro

Printed and bound by CPI Group (UK) Ltd, Croydon, CR0 4YY


ISBN 978 1913208 387


British Library Cataloguing in Publication Data.
A catalogue record for this book is available from the British Library.

So many books are dedicated to a single person that's been inspirational in that author's life. After reading this book you'll find out that I believe all of us are influenced by every event and person that we experience throughout the whole of our lives.

Therefore I'd like to dedicate *PEP Talk* to all of the friends and family members that have held my hand along the way and been my safety harness on the roller coaster of a ride that has been my life.

My children Harvey and Mimi, who've grown into wonderfully rounded, kind and supportive adults. I'm so proud of you both!

My wonderful partner Anna, who has helped me in so many ways that if I were to list them here the book would be twice as long.

I also dedicate this book to anyone that has ever known the torment of anxiety and want to let you all know, there is hope and help is out there!

# Foreword

The truth is, we can all become affected by the world and its contents and occasionally find ourselves in need of a 'pick-me-up' to make us feel better because often, life ain't no disco. This is a perfectly normal human reaction to some of the things in life that can make us feel down, because, after all, we're not coated in bubble wrap, are we?

We've all been through tough situations in life and all experienced the extraordinary power of hearing someone else's words that have made us look at things in a different light, making us feel so much better.

Most of us at some point have also found ourselves 'stuck in a rut' or found ourselves coasting through life where we put off things that are important to us, things that would deliver real benefits, but find ourselves doing something far more menial instead. Again, this is a perfectly normal thing for us to do as humans; our brains want to take us along the path of least resistance because changing things is a far more difficult proposition.

You know you want to change some things for the better, you know you put things off that would make you happier and even knowing these things you find yourself doing the same things you always do over and over again. It can often seem like the events of your life are taking you along a path that you wouldn't have chosen yourself. However, the truth is that until you receive your death sentence, there's really only one person in charge of your life: you!

What you need is something that gives you a little push or motivation to make some positive changes that not only take you away from lifes' annoyances but drive you towards the more positive things you want. That something is this book! You need a talking to that will be a stimulus to help you make the changes you want to not just pep you up but also provide you with the tools to make the changes.

So here's your PEP Talk!

# Contents

# Introduction

Picture a twelve-year-old boy with a mop of curly hair in his bedroom pretending to be asleep so as to make his father think he'd not been playing with his games rather than going to bed when he'd been told to. The boy could vaguely overhear an argument getting progressively more hostile coming from down the landing in his father's room. The boy was listening to a heated debate between his father and new stepmother, and the subject of the argument seemed to be about him.

The boy laid quietly and was a little upset listening to the antagonistic nature of the discussion, but then he heard his father shout, "Don't you dare tell him! If he ever found out it would break his heart." Right at that moment, the boy strangely somehow just knew what that meant.

About eighteen months earlier the young boy was devastated to have had lost his mum due to a heart attack brought on by angina and chronic high cholesterol; he was now living in a different house with his father and stepmother. The couple had been out for a meal with some of his father's old friends who'd known him for most of his life. During the meal the friends had broached a subject the boy's father wasn't prepared for and was extremely upset to have his new wife find out about the boy's true parentage.

That boy was me! My dad had been involved with a woman and had been unfaithful to my mum, or should I say the lady I had, up until the night of the argument, believed to be my mum. My dad had left the family home for about three years before I was born to live with the other woman and her existing children. Within that period of time I was conceived and then born in 1967. Approximately three years after my birth my dad took me away from my birth mother and reconciled his relationship with his wife. I never really understood why he made the decision to take me with him, but I think it was because he believed I'd have a better upbringing if he did. Apparently over a very short period of time I just took to calling my dad's wife 'Mum', copying my four older half-siblings who lived in the same house. For the sake of clarity, I will call my birth mother 'Mother' and my dad's wife 'Mum'.

As I grew up, I had no real recollection of my mother and was virtually completely oblivious living with my mum, dad and half-siblings, feeling, apart from the odd clue here and there, as though I was a normal child with nothing being different to the rest of my siblings. Really, how much does anyone remember about the first three or so years of their life? Compared to my half-siblings, there were subtle differences in my upbringing, though, which in some small way gave me tiny clues that something about me was different. For some reason, I had a very close bond with my mum and can still remember sitting next to her in the lounge watching the TV, holding her hand and twiddling with the rings on her fingers.

At this point I have to say, wow, what a woman! To take my dad back in after having an affair would have been emotionally difficult enough for her, but to also take in her husband's illegitimate child and treat them with such love and kindness is astounding. I think it was my dad's intense and pretty strict personality that not only made me very close to my mum but also stopped her, my half-siblings or anyone at all saying anything to me about my real origin.

Just to fill in some gaps, it might be important to explain that my dad had lived quite a hard life. He was a veteran of the Second World War, from which he'd developed 'shell shock' or what we might now call post-traumatic stress disorder (PTSD), which I'm confident was a contributing factor to his very strict parenting style.

With this being said, I'm sure you can imagine the emotional roller coaster I was on when I overheard the argument between my dad and my new stepmother; it's safe to say I was indeed heartbroken, as my dad had predicted.

I rarely share this story with anyone, not because I'm embarrassed, but because it doesn't seem a relevant thing to bring up in normal conversation. So why am I going public with this very personal story now?

The important word in my story is 'relevant', and it is the story's relevance to the content of this book that's made me decide to include it at all. That whole part of my life addresses many sections I cover in this book in order to provide you with an insight into how thinking differently means you have to challenge your own psychology so that you can benefit from this difference in the way you think about things. It wasn't long before overhearing the argument that I had to give up my belief in Santa Claus, but now I had to recognise the woman I'd believed was my mother now wasn't. The story is also relevant to the book because a lot of what I write about has often been called building 'psychological resilience', which is the ability to bounce back from adversity. It's also pertinent because it includes some very sad events, which I'm afraid to say most of us have either been through in our own pasts or may very well be likely to experience in the future and understanding our emotional response to that is important.

The upside to this story for me was that I was treated differently; my dad was strict but nothing like as strict with me as he was my older half-siblings, and I remember getting small gifts for no apparent reason from family members, for which at the time I didn't understand their motive but was always happy to receive. Today and, in fact, shortly after I found out about my mother, I was emotionally OK – that's the power of resilience when we're young. Unfortunately as we get older our thought processes become more rigid, making it tougher to bounce back, hence the reason for writing this book, to help you build in positive psychology so that when negative things do happen to you in life, you become more resilient to them. There is only one thing that, even after all this time, remains a great sadness for me and that is that I didn't know about my mother before my mum died and I never had the opportunity to thank my mum for taking me in, providing me with all that love and taking care of me so very wonderfully.

With all sincerity, your past can affect your psychology; I mean, of course it can, because, after all, every single thing you've done in your life up to this point has shaped who you are. We've all had successes and failures, experienced happiness and sadness, and experienced a number of surprises that life has a habit of delivering over and over again. We shouldn't, however, allow the negative events of the past affect our future potential happiness and while you can't physically change the things that have happened in your past, you can alter any negative impact these events may have on you for the future by changing the manner in which your memories are filtered.

OK, writing this book hasn't come easily to me, after all, 'I'm a talker and not a writer', so I've had to use every trick literally in *this* book to motivate myself to complete it.

The content of my training involves getting people to think about their own psychology and because of the introspective nature of it often makes people to look into the subject further. This interest in finding out more means that after my training sessions or at the end of conference talks, people have asked me hundreds of times if I have a book or delivered a TED talk, and I've always been a little bit embarrassed to say no. So I guess (at least at the time of publishing) I can now save fifty per cent of my blushes from this point forward.

I want to write this book differently; I want it to be heartfelt and real and, more than that, I want it to be a pragmatic help to you, the reader. I don't want it to be a styled 'self-help' book like some I've read that provide a good read but offer no long-lasting solutions to the problems a lot of people live with. I want it to provide genuine help that every person can benefit from in order to provide psychological resilience that improves personal positivity, self-empowerment and helps you perform better both personally and professionally, or in any way you find beneficial. With so much emphasis being placed on treating mental health issues recently, I want this to be a pioneering concept based on taking action to attempt to *prevent* mental health issues. Lastly, I'd like it to be a bestseller, but I guess positive psychology can only get you so far.

This book is based around some of the principals of something known as 'positive psychology', a means by which you focus on positive outcomes and positive things in order to build upon a way of thinking that provides greater creativity for problem-solving and to make you feel happier in different situations. It's about changing the preoccupation from just fixing what's wrong with psychological issues to paying more attention to building more on what's right with them. I have to point out at the start that positive psychology isn't about thinking positively all the time, suggesting you do wouldn't be accurate and might put some people off. If a piano is about to land on your head, thinking positively won't help, but looking for positive outcomes rather than focussing on your impending doom might help you consider how to think about positive solutions to your situation.

Can I begin by saying that what I'm talking about here isn't magic! Nobody can stop nasty people, bad things and uncomfortable events coming into your life; that's impossible. What this book and its contents can do, though, is to help you experience them differently, so these things don't have such a dramatic effect on you when they do come into your life. I want you to think about how different people are affected by events and people differently. Some people hate doing the ironing or cooking, for example. Others relish the idea of ploughing through a basket full of unironed clothes or spending time with ingredients in the kitchen. The tasks remain the same, so the variable in these situations is how every individual perceives the task differently. They've somehow developed methods to think of the task differently, as if they mentally filter the task so that when they think about it, their brain delivers a more positive emotional response. With this book I aim to show you how to build your own psychological PEP (Positivity – Empowerment – Performance) filters that can make people, events and situations seem different to you, better, or less annoying or stressful.

For a moment, can you think of a person that you have to deal with that you find difficult, unpleasant or an outright arseh*le (more about dealing with arseh*les later)? Really, take a moment to get a picture of that person in your head *now*. OK, now pop a big red, wobbly, elephant's trunk on their face where their nose should be. Can you see it? OK, now pop some big, floppy, red ears on them. Finally, hear them talking to you in a really silly voice that makes you smile.

Right, I want you to never, ever think of them like that again! You can't, can you? Once you've created an image in your mind of that person with those kind of changes, every time you think of them from now on, you'll think of them with the trunk, ears and funny voice. Guess what's going to happen the next time you see them? You'll be thinking of the new transformed person with the funny voice and you may even smile because you're thinking of them differently.

Think about what you've just done as creating a PEP filter, one single PEP filter for one annoying person. More about these PEP filters and how to create different ones for different people, events and tasks later.

I'm a psychologist and was previously in private practice as a psychotherapist, but this hasn't always been the case. When I began my working life, many, many years ago, I started in sales and marketing, and have held various positions with businesses large and small. In all my previous incarnations, I've not only had to motivate myself but other people too, and I'm proud to say that I became very good at working with many different types of personalities. It would be fair to say that I've developed a very optimistic outlook on life, but a few years ago while sitting at home watching the news, my partner said, "Ken, you're a misery!" Now I never thought of myself like that at all and it felt difficult to hear as it goes against my own internal identity, but after a short period of self-analysis I was confronted with the realisation that my partner was right. I was becoming a middle-aged Victor Meldrew. How could this be?

I'd been seeing a lot of clients with depression and anxiety just prior to this revelation and realised I was suffering with something known by psychotherapists as transference. This is where therapists, over time, begin to take on board the issues of their clients. It was time for action!

This transference was one of the reasons I began Tarragon Training, my training and public speaking business. Additionally, I'd come to realise that some of the techniques and skills I was using in private therapy with clients could be taught to anyone prior to them coming to see me, building a psychological resilience which could help them during stressful moments in their life.

Have you ever been so close to tears that you've really had to work hard to fight them back? Then, someone who's trying to help or is concerned with your well-being says to you, "Oh, are you all right?" You know what happens next: the floodgates open and all your emotions are released! I found with a lot of clients it usually, but not always, only took one small thing to push them over the edge and then found themselves in my practice room, as they couldn't resolve their issues on their own.

My aim with Tarragon Training and with this book is to help you use the skills and techniques I discuss later in order to prepare yourself for those times in the future when you might encounter frustrating people or negative events and experiences, so that you have the mental strength to deal with them differently and hopefully prevent you from needing professional help in the first place.

This book will show you how to exercise your brain by focussing on positive outcomes rather than dwelling on negative events or past memories of things that went wrong. The truth is you can't *not* exercise your brain; it's always exercising, taking in everything you experience, whether the experience is good, bad or indifferent. In fact, this exercise even takes place on a subconscious level while we're asleep and can alter our views about aspects of our lives. Have you ever had a dream about a person you know that when you wake up has changed how you feel about them? In reality, nothing has actually changed about them at all, but you've somehow managed to change your emotional response to that person simply because of what happened in your dream. Essentially, you've installed a filter in your brain that now makes you feel different when you think about them. We all learn to filter the world in different ways based upon our individual experiences of life and how we've interpreted them, or filtered them. Sometimes these filters aren't helpful because they cause us to feel negative about aspects of our lives which inhibit positive outcomes.

So why not focus on positive outcomes in every situation? Just think about how your brain makes your whole body feel when you think about bad or negative things and then how it feels when you think about good or positive things. How would you prefer to feel? So let's focus on positive outcomes... this book could be good and maybe even change your life!

In order for you to get real benefits from this book, I have to show you how important it is to change beliefs and habits. Again, I know from experience how difficult it is for people to change these things; in fact it's incredibly difficult, for scientific reasons which I'll talk a little more about later.

I do need you to do some things differently, though, so let's start with habits. What do you normally drink first thing in the morning? Tea, coffee or something else? Right, from now on I'd like you to swap. If you normally drink tea, I want you to change and drink coffee, or if its coffee you normally drink, I want you to swap and start drinking tea. How does that feel? Uncomfortable, right?

I've asked literally thousands of people to do this during my talks and because of this have become aware that lots of people will be thinking that your morning drink selection is a preference and not a habit. I want to prove that it's a habit. Most people, not everyone, have at some point had an alcoholic drink in our lives. Can you remember the first time you had that first drink? In a lot of cases it was when we were young and might have been a little sip of our parents' wine or beer. When you had that first sip, was it nice?

The answer in most cases is 'NO!' But... you cracked on with that habit, didn't you?!

Still not convinced? OK then, try swapping the side of the bed you usually sleep on. Even though it's just a habit, a lot of people will find that swapping sides of the bed is even more difficult to do than changing your morning drinking habit and even begin throwing out excuses, saying they might swap sides but their partner won't or even say they can't swap because they're closer to the window or something. This is what I mean about how difficult it is to change habits; it's really hard. Even though I've told you to change one of these habits because it will bring benefits for the way you think, it's doubtful that you'll change, right? In reality, all I'm really asking you to do is move three feet across the bedroom this evening.

But as I've said, it isn't just about changing habits, it's also about changing beliefs, which are equally tough, if not tougher to change. During my talks I often ask people to raise their hands if they believe they have a perfect body. How many people do you think raise their hands? Hardly anyone does, and when I get that rare person who actually does raise their hand, they often only do it as a joke among their peers. I then go on to ask them to raise their hands again if they believe they're attractive. I usually get a tiny number of confident people show me their hands, but it is only a tiny number. The truth is, we're all attractive in some way, right? I mean, everyone at some point has attracted someone else, ergo, we're all attractive. Whether that attraction was wanted or not, it's happened. What's happening here is that either they believe they're attractive but can't raise their hands for fear of repercussion in people's opinion of them afterwards or they genuinely don't believe it, in which case, they're incorrect. Limiting beliefs like these do not support positive mental health and we need to begin considering changing them. By the way... I have a perfect body!

Now you may well have certain thoughts about what I've just said, but if I was genuine with that statement and really believed it because I think it makes me happier, what's it got to do with you?

I'm not suggesting you start going around telling everyone you have a perfect body; society isn't ready for you and your new belief. You can, however, begin 'thinking' more positive things about yourself and start feeling the benefits. I'm working on the presumption throughout this book that you, the reader, are working with a normally functioning psychology, are doing your best in your work and social life, and are not an advocate for hurting small animals and children. If that's the case, that you're doing your best and consider yourself a good person on the whole, then why shouldn't you start believing better things about yourself and telling yourself these things in your head. By the way, if you say nice things to yourself about yourself in your head... nobody can hear you!

But it's not just about you. I'm an advocate for treating people with compassion and kindness, and would encourage us all to help each other more. This isn't just because I'm soppy. It's because I know from experience how great it feels when someone's helped me. This help can be in multiple forms that take shape as things like random acts of kindness or simply saying something nice to someone else.

Some time ago, I noticed a guy in the middle of my home city centre that was just standing there with a small sign hanging around his neck. As I got closer to him, I could see everyone avoiding him and initially thought he was one of the dozens of poor homeless people I'd already seen that day. When I got close to him, I could make out what it said on his sign and it simply read 'Please Help'.

I decided to talk to him to see what the problem was. I asked him if everything was OK and he informed me he was blind and trying to find his way to the broadband shop. He was literally less than thirty metres away, so I offered him help; he took my arm and we walked into the shop. I explained to the person behind the counter that the gentleman was blind and that he needed help with his broadband. After I'd done this, the man went on to thank me 'profusely'; I mean, he was extraordinarily grateful and made sure the whole shop knew that he thought I'd been so amazing in my help. His words 'built up' the thirty metre walk I'd helped him with so much that at one point I thought the whole shop was going to spontaneously erupt with applause for what I'd done. I'm sure you can imagine who got the most from that whole interaction: me! I felt great for the rest of the day, even though I'd done a tiny thing to help.

Events like these are good for you. The very simple act of saying something nice to someone or providing a tiny act of random kindness will not only build your own self-esteem but also improve your positive psychology.

My aim with this book is to take you through a process of understanding how the world and its contents can sometimes affect you in negative ways through something called transference, how your beliefs about yourself and the world can generate both negative and positive emotions that often seem outside our conscious control, and how your habits become part of who you are, whether good or bad.

Then I want to explain how our brains interpret the outside world through our senses and how these sensory stimuli can be reprogrammed to produce positive rather than negative emotional responses. I want to give you an insight into how to deal with difficult people because, let's face it, they exist, and you may not be able to change them, but you should be able to have strategies to deal with them so they don't affect you negatively.

Finally, I'm going to show you how to filter the world in a different way so that you can focus more on the good stuff in your life and have the bad stuff not feel so bad. That would be nice, wouldn't it?

# Chapter One

# Transference

## (How the World Affects You)

So I'd begun to take on the symptoms of my clients; luckily I had the knowledge to change what I was becoming and get myself back on the right track before I became a permanent grump. Through delivering training courses to lots of organisations around the country, I've noticed that lots of people work in very stressful jobs or are in environments where they're having to deal with difficult, confrontational or emotional situations.

Most of my psychotherapy work was thoroughly enjoyable and I had lots of success working with some lovely people whom I'd been fortunate enough to be able to help change for the better. Since starting my training business some years ago, however, I've become aware that some of the NHS staff, council workers, social workers and lots of others I've trained are constantly dealing with difficult situations, which means they're subjecting themselves to environmental influences which can have an adverse effect on their own mental health. Personally, I do all I can to avoid these negative environments, but some people, because of the nature of where their work takes them, can't; they're putting themselves in horrible situations and environments on purpose!

A long time ago, I used to work in the fire alarm industry, and you may or may not be aware that some manufacturing industries have to take unique and specific actions in order to protect themselves. In places where they're manufacturing products where lots of fine particles are produced on purpose or as a by-product of the manufacturing process, they can be susceptible to explosions. These explosions occur due to the tiny sparks that occur when an electrical switch is operated, because it ignites the fine powder in the environment. Any device that has the potential to produce a tiny spark has to be made 'intrinsically safe', meaning that every device has to be securely sealed such that when a spark occurs it's kept inside the device and the fine powder can't ignite. The intention of this book is to provide you with the knowledge that can keep you as intrinsically safe from your environment as possible.

We can all be affected by our environments, so if you spend your time working in an organisation where morale is low or you live with someone miserable, you can easily, quickly and totally subconsciously 'transfer' this to your own emotional condition.

Think of it a little like 'catching an accent'. If you moved to America from the UK, over time you'd begin to talk with American tones and use American words. You wouldn't turn up on day one and instantly talk with an American accent; that would be odd! The environment slowly slips into your subconscious actions as you consciously notice the differences and begin to blend in.

The same thing applies with feelings, actions and emotions. Unfortunately, these feelings, actions and emotions become habitual to the point that they become part of your belief system and ultimately form and mould your identity. Occasionally during training, I've had people saying to me, "Ken, I like being miserable." The misery has become their identity and they now not only see themselves as miserable but also feel uncomfortable changing the habit of misery they've built. When this happens, I kind of want to shake them and say, "It's not all about you, is it? What about all the other people around you that you're infecting with your misery?" You'll know only too well what this feels like if you live with someone miserable. I want you to think of emotional transference as if it were a virus. Constantly surrounding yourself with negative emotions can virally affect your own mental condition almost as if you'd caught the flu, but with longer term repercussions. Around the world we have different cultures that impact on the way we interact in those societies and also affect our attitude.

For example, I lived in America for a few years and noticed a difference in people's attitudes towards other people's success and failure. I can't lump every person from every culture into different groups because we're all different, but in my experience in the USA I genuinely found most people looked at things differently to the way a lot of us British people do. On the first day of my arrival in New Jersey, I arrived at our new offices with my new business partner. As we pulled up outside the office, we noticed a lady driving a Ferrari arrive and park in the space next to us. She got out of the car and walked towards her offices, displaying drippings of wealth: designer suit, expensive handbag and lots of jewellery, you get the picture. My new American business partner turned to me and said, "Wow, did you see that, Ken? That's awesome, she's achieved so much, I wonder how she's managed to do that." In my mind, I was thinking, if I were back in England that's not what most of us British people would be thinking! Isn't it true that so many of us would have thought almost exactly the opposite?

It's almost as though the virility of our cultures has 'transferred' into our subconscious thoughts.

There is good news, thankfully. The truth is that if negativity can be transferred, then so can positivity. Surrounding yourself with as much positivity and happiness in your environment will help you subconsciously transfer yourself into a more positive, happier person. As I've already said at the outset, bad things, difficult people and negative events will happen, but not focussing on them will help your psychology become more positive. Please don't think I'm suggesting you forget about the bad things; you won't be able to, anyway, and you'll still have to deal with them. I just don't want these negative thoughts to be your default thought processes, because we all know how they make us feel physically. People will tell you that I regularly tell conference audiences that if they're going to sit there throughout my talk and be miserable then that's fine, but I'm not going to look at them! And, I don't, I'm looking at the ninety-nine per cent who are enjoying what I'm saying, smiling and laughing. I mean, honestly, why would I want to focus on the one per cent who don't want to become engaged or enjoy their day? I want the majority of the audiences' positivity and happiness to transfer to me and repel the negativity. I know it's there; any public speaker will tell you that we do notice the miseries, I just choose not to focus on them, and I strongly advocate you try to do the same in whatever situation you're in.

I've met lots of people who work in training and as such, I know we all receive feedback from our sessions letting the person who's commissioned the training know how effective or enjoyable it's been and whether the training was value for money. The feedback we receive is obviously valuable, because we all like to believe we're doing a good job and are able to make changes where necessary in order to improve. I regularly receive very positive feedback from my sessions, but I can tell you that every trainer, no matter how engaging and interesting their training is, will at some point read comments that aren't complimentary about their work. Because of the subject matter of my training, people who train in different disciplines often ask me about how to deal with this negative feedback. A lot of these other trainers often work with groups of around forty or so people and go on to tell me about the one person who's said something negative. They tell me the feedback was simply negative, not constructive in any way and felt there was nothing different they could have done to change their content which would have made a difference. They focus emotionally on that one single comment, while placing much less emphasis on the other thirty-nine glowing comments. Their psychology makes them consider their training performance more because of the one poor comment, so I strongly encourage them to alter their thoughts to spend more time considering the positive feedback and treat it proportionally rather than allowing the minority view transfer to them. The old adage is correct: you can't please all of the people all of the time.

So, if you suddenly find yourself thinking far more negative thoughts than positive ones, the first thing you should look at is your environment and question how or why these negative processes might be being transferred.

# Chapter Two

# Placebo vs Nocebo

I would imagine that most people reading this would be familiar with the concept of a placebo and its use, but equally believe that most people wouldn't know about the principles of 'nocebo' – my spell checker isn't even recognising the word.

Essentially, a placebo has historically been used in medicine to test the efficacy of real drugs. In drug testing there would be two groups of people: one group would be given the real drug and the other group given sugar pills (the placebo), with no one knowing if they're taking the real drug or the sugar pill. Many results would be recorded to see how each person in both groups reacts to the pills they've been taking. In theory the group taking the real drug should notice some benefits from taking their medicine and the placebo group should have no benefit at all. However, over and over again medical trials have demonstrated that a good number of those taking the sugar pill noticed positive benefits and the whole subject of placebos is constantly being researched to find out ways in which this psychological process can be enhanced to help us in a variety of situations.

By the way, in tests where a group takes the placebo, they regularly show signs of the side effects listed on the back of the packet of the real drug, which is providing a negative outcome – the opposite of placebo, nocebo!

The BBC TV programme *Horizon* produced an excellent show around placebos and their effect on people where some of the GB cycling teams were told they were being given harmless, legal, performance-enhancing drugs which should improve their times around the circuit. In almost every case, the cyclists' times showed significant improvement even though they were actually only given placebos. If you can find the programme anywhere on catch up, I would highly recommend the show.

So if a placebo is a substance or process with no medically beneficial content that's delivered to a person but still produces positive effects, then we can say the same but opposite for nocebos. The key word here is 'process', and I don't want you to think of a placebo as a pill but more as a process which produces a positive, beneficial outcome. It's my contention that if we can be given sugar pills that produce positive benefits despite our not knowing whether or not these pills are 'real' medicine, then we can provide ourselves with psychological processes that do the same, which is, in fact, the main purpose of this book, and the means by which I do that is to teach you how to install PEP filters, which I explain later.

This brings me on to a well-documented, strange but true story about a guy called Vance Vanders. I'd like to emphasise that this is a true story which you can research yourself on the internet and the story has been corroborated and published in medical journals. When I tell this story, I like to use a little artistic storytelling creativity, so the precise details may vary a tiny bit, but the fundamentals of the story remain the same.

Sometime in 1937, Vance decided to walk home one night through an Alabama graveyard. While walking through the dark cemetery, he came across a witch doctor and, for whatever reason, there ensued an argument between them. The argument culminated in the witch doctor grabbing Vance by the face. At this point, the witch doctor reached into his coat pocket, pulling out a glass vile which he proceeded to waft under Vance's nose and said, "I've just put a curse on you; you're going to die a horrible, painful death and there's nothing you can do about it." After the confrontation, Vance then continued his walk home and when he arrived, described to his wife exactly what had happened to him in the cemetery. Vance went to bed and woke up several hours later with excruciating stomach pains. Over the next few hours the pains got worse and worse, to the point that Vance's wife had him admitted to hospital. Upon his arrival at the hospital, the doctors and nurses examined him, and guess what? That's right, none of them could find a single cause for Vance's pain. The pain was getting progressively worse and more sustained over time, when finally, after months of suffering in hospital – I imagine out of desperation – Vance's wife decided to speak to the head doctor, Dr Doherty. She explained to the doctor precisely what had happened to Vance in the graveyard.

At first the doctor was sceptical, but after consideration and with the realisation that nothing the hospital had done so far was helping Vance at all, Doherty decided to try something. The following morning, Doherty walked into Vance's room, where I'm sure you can picture the scene. All of Vance's family were there, his wife crying, expecting Vance to die at any moment, with Vance himself writhing in agony on the bed. Doherty announced to the room that the previous evening he'd visited the graveyard himself and had been able to speak with the witch doctor personally. He said, "Listen, Vance, I've found out what the witch doctor has done to you. Basically, he infected you when he wafted that glass vile under your nose, because inside that bottle were lizard eggs, and somehow during your confrontation you ingested what was inside the bottle. You've ingested a lizard egg, the egg has hatched and now the lizard is trying to eat its way out of you." Doherty then reached into his medical bag and very ceremoniously produced a large syringe, which contained a drug the doctor knew would make Vance vomit.

He proceeded to inject Vance with the contents of the syringe, explaining to Vance that the drug would make him vomit and whatever was inside of him would come out. Doherty left the room for a few moments in order for the drug to take effect. On his return, Vance was being violently sick and at this point the doctor placed his bag on the floor next to where Vance had been vomiting. While Vance wasn't looking, Doherty reached into his bag and pulled out a lizard he'd placed there earlier and held it up in the air, announcing, "*Aha*, look, Vance, this was what was causing you all the pain, it's out now, you're cured!" Vance fell back on the bed and went to sleep, waking up several hours later, when he felt absolutely fine. As the story goes, from that point on Vance lived happily ever after. To this day, voodoo is still practised in some of the southern parts of the USA.

So my question to you is, was this actually voodoo or was it a nocebo?

You know how it makes you feel when someone says something nice to you, pays you a compliment that you appreciate or tells you you've done something well; you feel good, don't you? All they're really doing is giving you a little placebo which delivers a positive emotion for you. Now think about someone you love or trust, someone important whose opinion you value, says something like, "Oh dear, you do look peaky today." Almost immediately after that you'd be internally questioning if you actually do feel peaky and the sensation delivers a negative emotion for you, a nocebo.

So we need to be careful with nocebos, because they aren't always delivered to us on purpose or by design; they're sneaky, and I believe we're surrounded by them. It's easy to see why, all you need to do is watch the news this evening or read a newspaper and you'll notice virtually all of what you're seeing or hearing is negative. I mean really, how many times do you need to see a plane fly into a building before you get the message about what's happened? If you were around at the time of the 9/11 plane attacks on the New York World Trade Center, you'll remember how many times the crashes were replayed, over and over again. When your brain is overwhelmingly receiving these negative signals over and over again, it will very quickly begin to become confused over the ratio of good to bad in the world. We know that negative environments create stress, which is harmful to physical health, and allowing yourself to be surrounded by negative stories or events place you in a negative environment. If you, like me, believe that there's a yin to every yang in the world, then it seems obvious that positive environments create resilience, which is why I'm strongly suggesting that you watch out for the thousands of nocebos we're surrounded by and pay more attention to the placebos, which are unfortunately provided much less often.

I'm not suggesting you give up on current affairs if that's something that's important to you, but I would mention that occasionally I meet people that no longer watch the TV news or read newspapers and I've found them to be some of the happiest people I meet.

As if these nocebos that surround us are not enough to have a negative effect on us, we can also often be prone to provide our own by repeating negative things about ourselves in our own head: self-nocebos! When we make mistakes, it can become a habit to continually reprimand ourselves, affirming how bad we are at certain tasks. When you think about it, this is the worst kind of nocebo, I mean, it's *you* telling *you* you're no good or rubbish, of course you're going to listen to that.

Over the years I've been fortunate enough to have worked with some top sportspeople, some of whom have developed a very bad habit of repeated self-nocebo. I've known footballers, for example, who constantly reprimand themselves when they miss a shot on goal, or golfers who openly demonstrate their disappointment in themselves by throwing their clubs or putting their heads down. If you continue to supply yourself with self-nocebos, of course you're going to begin to build a belief that you're going to mess up again next time. This is likely the cause for top football strikers going through what they call 'goal droughts'. They're not expecting to score because of what they continue to say to themselves about themselves in their head. Furthermore, they say these things so much that when they eventually do score, they think it's a fluke and expect to miss the next shot. These negative affirmations, that aren't limited to footballers, will obviously alter your behaviour.

Rather than saying things to yourself like, "I can't score goals," or, "I always mess that up," you'd be much better served by using positive psychology and telling yourself, "Next time I'll score!" or, "I'll get that right next time!"

Most workplaces have regular meetings where they discuss issues that have gone wrong. They'll discuss how it went wrong, why it went wrong and try to attribute what was responsible for the error in the first place. This is good for correcting problems and is probably a necessary process. However, if they had regular meetings with people from different parts of the business that discussed only the things they've done that have gone right and produced positive outcomes, they might have learnt from other people how to do something correctly in the first place, which would remove the necessity for the meeting to discuss where something went wrong. Unfortunately, most of our workplaces don't operate like this and I've worked with lots of organisations that cause their employees to live in fear of making mistakes rather than focussing on the things that work well.

I believe that when we work in a happy, pleasant environment, we're not only far more productive but also much more creative; as we know, our brains have been scientifically proven to work better when we think more positively. To some people, the very thought of going to work on a Monday morning causes them to feel awful, so just thinking of their workplace is a nocebo. However, when they think about the upcoming weekend, they'll begin to feel good and the thought of the weekend is a placebo.

So it's my contention that, if you have to work and you, for whatever reason, can't find a job you enjoy doing more, you have two choices. You can continue allowing the nocebo provided by the thought of where you work affect you negatively, or you change the way you think about your workplace. I know that me simply saying that to you doesn't help; in fact, if it was as easy as that then this would be a very short book indeed, so you'll be happy to hear that I've included the PEP filter chapter, which explains exactly how you can make things like this seem better and have them affect you less negatively.

At this stage, you probably have no idea how that whole process is possible, or dislike your workplace so much that just believe the depth of thought you have about it wouldn't change, no matter what I told you. There are thousands of psychotherapists all over the country that actively help people with incredibly serious issues and they constantly help people feel better about their problems. In the knowledge that psychotherapy processes help *these* people, then if you follow the methods I lead you through later, then these processes can certainly help you feel happier about your workplace.

## Chapter Three

# The Importance of Silliness

Look, so many people work in environments where being professional has, over the years, turned them into being sternly serious about everything all the time, and I've had personal experience working at organisations like this where their culture has created a very serious but demoralised workforce. Over time, these cultures have developed such that the seriousness becomes natural which nurtures poor morale and, because of this, cause stress among their employees. Over the years, I've experienced lots of workplaces like this and the atmosphere is almost tangible the moment you walk through the front door.

I'm sure that you wouldn't behave in the same way I have in the past, but I can tell you there have been times in the past when I've genuinely dreaded the thought of going to work because of the negative nature of the culture. I confess there have been times when I've picked up the telephone in the morning, called my workplace and while putting on my best 'croaky' voice, my side of the conversation would have sounded something like this:

"Hello?"

*Cough*

"Sorry, I won't be in today."

*Sniff*

"Err, the flu, I think."

*Nose blow*

"I might be in on Friday."

*Cough*

"Sorry!"

What I can also tell you is that the very moment I put the phone down, I actually began to question my health and started to actually feel a little poorly; I'd nocebo'd myself!

Most people enjoy having fun and laughing; we may all have different senses of humour but almost everyone feels good when someone or something makes us smile and laugh. Happiness is, in fact, our ultimate motivator as human beings and while we're all motivated to do lots of things, ultimately we're doing them to make us happy.

Let me ask you a question. When you've been at home all alone, have you ever been known to do silly things because nobody is watching? If you can answer yes, then you'll know that when you do these silly things it's a light-hearted relief for the day and it makes you feel good. Singing into a hairbrush or dancing around your living room feels good and makes you smile. However, because of social convention and the subsequent potential feeling of embarrassment, we don't do these silly things in public. Occasionally, though, sometimes people get caught out and it's wonderful!

We've all been in a car, pulled up to the traffic lights and seen the misery on the face of the driver of the car next to you. Then there's the rare case where you pull up to the traffic lights, look over at the driver next to you, and you'll see them singing at the top of their lungs and impersonating the person singing on the radio. At that point something wonderful happens... they catch you looking at them!

Right at that moment, you're both smiling or laughing at the situation, and that makes your day.

We know that seeing someone do something silly diminishes the seriousness of your day and makes you happy, so why aren't we doing more silly things like this when we know it makes us and others feel good? To prove my point, I'm going to offer up a confession. I hesitate to make this admission public as I don't want you to tut and put the book down because I've gone down in your estimation. While I have made this confession previously during training sessions, it's not something I include routinely, so I will usually only do this with the most smiley audiences.

But if I'm genuinely wanting you to get over your embarrassment and introduce the importance of silliness into your lives, I have no choice but to share with you a 'thing' that I do that I've previously only shared with a rare few. OK, here goes, are you ready for this?

*I slap chickens in Sainsburys!*

Take a moment to absorb that for a while.

Previously when I've told people that, they take a moment before asking why. I do it because it causes a positive reaction from others. My partner and kids always laugh when I do it. They don't even have to be on the same aisle to know I've done it because they can hear it. The reaction from strangers varies from laughing out loud to smiling through to generating a slight head tilt that you'd usually only see on a curious dog. In any case, I know that when they get home they're in for the 'You'll never guess what I've just seen at the supermarket' conversation with their family. That always makes me smile. I'm spreading happiness using silliness.

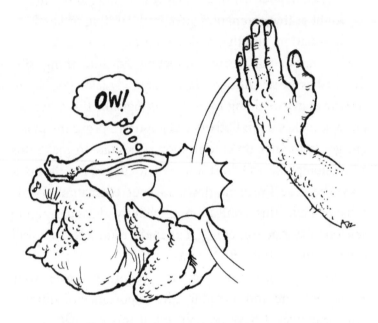

For those of a sensitive nature, have confidence that if you buy supermarket chickens that they won't be 'pre-slapped' by me; I always buy the chickens I've slapped for my own consumption. Additionally, this is *my* silly thing, so please don't start doing this too; I don't want to start an epidemic of chicken slapping, find your own silliness!

Silliness is important, because if you look at the world through most of our media, you'll see war, anxiety, negative events and serious issues which your brain will soon begin to let its attention become biased towards, making you believe that the majority of the world is this way. This is called 'attentional bias' and I talk a little more about this later. Silliness can be used in certain thought processing techniques in order to help reduce the significance of negative memories and, again, I'll explain more about this later.

For most, but not all of us, childhood is a happy, carefree part of our life, and as children we were often silly. This attitude to being silly is gradually educated out of us into adulthood, where we're supposed to 'act like grown-ups' or 'be professional'. I wonder if you ever got told off by your parents when you were younger and got told to, "Stop showing off!", which, by the way, they only did just because of their own embarrassment. Think about that for a moment: just prior to you being told off for showing off, what was happening to you? You were probably being silly or just having fun, right? So my question is, what message do you think your little brain took from that statement from your parents? Yep, it wasn't stop showing off, it was stop being silly and stop having fun!

You'll be aware of many times in your life where the seriousness of some situations cause you to become stressed and if you're lucky you may remember a time when the horrible atmosphere that's been created was significantly reduced with levity or silliness. Many years ago, while I was working for an organisation in the fire industry, me, my boss and two colleagues were driving along Hollywood Boulevard in Los Angeles, trying desperately to find a Jewish restaurant to eat at. Our boss had arranged to take a very important potential client to dinner and the contract's potential value was enormous. All of us were aware that our boss was becoming increasingly agitated and stressed knowing the client would only eat kosher food, and we'd spent an hour looking for a suitable restaurant to eat at, but we weren't having any luck at all. This was before the time of the smartphone, which would have made the whole search much easier, but we had to search the old-fashioned way.

My two other colleagues weren't truly aware about quite how serious this situation was, how important landing this contract was and how many jobs depended on it. They just noticed the terrible atmosphere building in the car as the boss got more upset about this predicament. Every couple of minutes one of my colleagues, who was actually just hungry, kept saying, "How about that place, boss?", which was countered by the boss saying, "*No, that one's no good!*" This was followed by the other colleague saying, "That restaurant looks all right, what about that?", and again the boss shouted, "*No, we've got to find the right place!*" This whole thing was building and building over the course of about an hour, with the comments coming from the back of the car and them pointing out unsuitable restaurants, which was met with increasingly angry comments back from the boss, whose driving was becoming erratic due to his anxiety. At the height of the boss's anxiety, one of the backseat drivers finally said, "Look, boss, that place over there looks great, is that one OK?" The boss replied, with incredulity, "*For heaven's sake, no! Do you want to keep your job? I've told you, it has to be kosher!*" I honestly thought the boss was going to fire him there and then, and I can tell you we were all getting so stressed that we'd have been useless in a meeting with the client at this point anyway. The colleague who'd received the telling off then decided to come back at him with this: "Listen, boss, it might not be kosher but I'm sure it'll be cushty."

There was a short moment of silence, followed by the whole car erupting in laughter. I'm sure you can imagine how the whole atmosphere was lifted because of this silly comment; the boss calmed down and was able to think more clearly, remembering someone he could call to find a suitable restaurant, while his driving improved significantly. We did eventually find a kosher restaurant, met the client and won the contract. Removing the negative emotion from the situation through the application of a little silliness made everyone feel better and able to think more creatively; we became relaxed and comfortably able to deal with the client in a calm relaxed manner. Can you imagine how stressed we'd have been trying to work with the client, had we eventually invited him to dine with us and not had a chance to improve the atmosphere between us with silliness?

Silliness is, of course, totally subjective and is dependent upon your own personality and sense of humour which has developed in a unique way for you based upon your own upbringing and life experiences. So if you don't find my examples funny, that's fine, but do find your own and build them into your life so you can help yourself diminish the seriousness that a lot of the things you'll experience can generate. It's important to recognise the seriousness of a lot of situations you'll find yourself in, but I don't want you to find yourself enveloped by it, because allowing this to happen can not only affect your own psychology but can also negatively impact others around you.

Someone close to me told me a story which demonstrated

really well how silliness can help others becoming affected by their behaviour. When they were a child, they remembered how their mother would always cower whenever there was a thunderstorm and how the fear brought on by the thunder would force her to hunker down in the corner of the room protecting herself. Their mother recognised how this could have a negative effect on the children and used to say with a smile, "Oh dear, look at Mum being so silly." The mother knew that by telling her kids that she was being silly, it would diminish the seriousness of the situation. The sort of repeated behaviour the mother demonstrated to her kids could have had long-term phobic repercussions for them, but this wasn't passed on to her kids because of her silly reactions. I explain more about this in the 'Changing Your Existing Filters into PEP Filters' chapter.

When we're being silly, scientifically what happens is that neurotransmitters in our brains produce dopamine and serotonin, which are chemicals connected to our brains 'pleasure centre'. Both these chemicals produce some very positive effects for us. They both improve our 'learning memory' and, between them, cause us to think with more clarity, make us more motivated and deliver feelings of relaxation so we become less stressed. There are many positive effects that the production of these chemicals can have on us and they're an important part of good mental health that, when functioning normally, can not only make us feel better but also keep us away from depression and anxiety.

So, I'm claiming back silliness; it's just too important to leave in childhood, it harms nobody, it doesn't make you any less professional and it makes you smile, feel good and, moreover, makes other people smile too.

## Chapter Four

# Your Beliefs

Firstly, let's start this section by saying that beliefs aren't real, they're just a thing! Obviously, beliefs are powerful and often guide our behaviour to make us do the most extraordinary things because they can *seem* very real. Being real and seeming real though are very different things. Most of us believed in Santa Claus when we were kids. Do you remember that almost nuclear explosion level of excitement you used to get at the thought of Santa arriving with the presents? Of course, when we get older, the belief goes and the excitement diminishes.

Think about this for a moment. When we get older, most of us lose that physical level of excitement, but if you can still remember what that felt like, then wouldn't you like that feeling back again? We learn how to feel different, losing a wonderful sensation, which for most people is only ever noticed again the moment we have young children of our own and begin to feel these sensations vicariously through our kids. As they get older, we lose it again. So potentially you still have the ability to think about things that would, in the past, have generated wonderful sensations inside you and regain them.

Now I'm not saying that if a belief serves you well you should change it. It's those beliefs we have that hold us back or don't serve us well I'm targeting and want you to reconsider. If you have a limiting belief, it will limit your behaviour. Consider this: I've always had the greatest admiration for Olympic gold medal winners, particularly, for me, winter Olympic gold medal winners. Whenever I see them there up on the podium singing out to their national anthem, I get an enormous sense of pride and a tinge of envy. I would, in my life, have genuinely loved to have achieved something so amazing to me and be the recipient of a gold medal. I often ask people if they think I could win a gold medal and the question is usually followed by silence as they look at my balding head and fifty-two-year-old body.

The truth is, maybe I could win a gold medal in a sport that's not too energetic like, let's say, curling. Now I'm not saying people who curl at the top of their sport don't need to be physically fit, of course they do. But I have seen older competitors nearing my age when I've watched the sport before, so it would be fair to say that there's an outside chance I could indeed win a gold medal. Having said this, 'I believe' that if I were to have any chance at all of winning one of these medals I covet so much, I'd have to dedicate virtually all of my life to practise and competitive curling, leaving little to no time for anything else in my life. So guess what? I don't even curl for fun, in fact I've never thrown a stone! My limiting belief has limited my behaviour. I may have a natural talent for curling and maybe I wouldn't have to give up everything else in my life to have a chance of winning, but I don't believe that (more about this in the 'Nature vs Nurture' chapter).

I've seen so many private clients that don't believe certain positive things about themselves or their lives and these limiting beliefs have gone on to negatively affect their mental health. Some of these people don't believe they can be happy, they don't believe they're strong enough, they don't believe they're loveable, and many other limiting beliefs like these. Changing them is difficult, because most of these beliefs have been supported by lots of different events in their lives which they focus on as evidence for their belief. Just because these beliefs are difficult to change doesn't mean they can't be; it's often the case of them noticing things in their life that don't support what they believe, breaking their psychological programme of behavioural response. One of my aims with this book is to have you focus more on positive things that are in your world; don't worry about the consequences of not focussing on the bad things, they'll happen anyway and just because you're not focussing on them doesn't mean you won't have to deal with them – you will have to. I know from experience that looking for positive outcomes in difficult situations allows you the opportunity to be far more creative in finding solutions to the problem, rather than by simply considering all the potential negative outcomes; you'll think about these anyway.

I've known so many people who've not even attempted to try something they've always wanted to do due to their belief that the outcomes will be negative as they've been before for them, as if they're telling their own fortune. It's these beliefs I want to address with this book and even as I write this sentence I'm aware that any reader who has a firm belief that self-help style books don't help, they'll struggle to benefit from my suggestions. As a psychologist, I know why these beliefs are held on to with such vigour and passion, often denying logic, evidence and any potentially beneficial results.

Throughout my life I've come across people with what I consider to be very strange beliefs, take superstitions, for example. In my opinion, superstitions occur or are supported because of what is known as a person's 'internal' or 'external' locus of control. This theory says that if you have an internal locus of control then you believe you're in control of your own life, and if you have an external locus of control then you believe your life is in the control of outside factors. Superstitions suggest that certain events will happen in people's lives because of apparently unrelated occurrences. Does something bad happen to you every Friday 13th? If it historically has, then I've lost you at this point, but there will be some superstitions you believe in and others you don't, so you're being selective about which ones you decide to believe in and which ones you don't. What about breaking a mirror, seeing a black cat or touching wood? How can seeing a black cat logically bring you bad luck, and if it did, does that mean that people who live with them as pets spend their whole lives suffering through a series of unfortunate events? I think superstitious people are becoming biased to look for things they believe in, and I explain this in the 'Attentional Bias and Motivation' chapter. Seriously, though, if you are fanatically superstitious, please don't put this book down yet; there's lots of other stuff you might agree with.

Truthfully, though, people are at liberty to believe in whatever they want, regardless of whether it fits into my belief system or not. If I'm honest, I've historically held a couple of very odd beliefs myself. Many years ago, I worked for a very charismatic boss who, in many ways, mentored me and helped me progress in my career. Due to the respect I had for him, I'd regularly take up a number of his business ideas and philosophies, most of which were helpful and just. One day, however, during an important meeting with a business associate in which my boss was present, we noticed how slippery the business associate was becoming and we knew he wasn't being honest with us. The business associate had a first name and a surname that could also be given as a first name. My boss suggested a break in the meeting and took me aside away from the meeting room to have a chat with me. My boss said, "Ken, do you notice he's being selective with the truth?" I answered, "Yes!" My boss then announced, in all seriousness, "Right, let's get back into the meeting, but let me tell you, Ken – you should never trust a man with two first names!" For years after that, it became a belief of mine, totally illogical, but whenever I met a 'Peter Edwards' or 'John Phillips' I'd have an instant subconscious negative emotional response, that thankfully I later realised that that was ridiculous. I'm aware how absurd that sounds, but the origin of the belief came from someone respected and trusted, so I was sold on it, and it affected my emotions and behaviour.

I've already said that lots of us will find some others' beliefs difficult to understand and occasionally even feel a little uncomfortable around people who hold different beliefs to our own. I'm really only concerned about beliefs that don't serve people well and where they hold on to them for dear life, even though they recognise the belief is, in some way, serving them poorly. It can be baffling trying to understand these beliefs and why someone would want to continue to follow them, and in fact you may never completely understand the logic behind some of them. However, we know in psychotherapy there's something known as 'secondary gain', which explains why people can't or won't change something about themselves that would improve their lives. I've worked with people in the past that have eventually spoken about how their issue affects them incredibly badly, but if they were able to overcome the problem, they'd lose something more important in their life. For example, if they no longer had the issue, they might lose the attention from their family members that they believe they only receive because of their suffering from the issue in the first place. So if they lost the issue, they'd then lose the attention paid to them by the family, making it more important for them to keep the negative issue.

Secondary gain occurs in many different aspects of life and you'd think, for example, that every criminal wouldn't want to get caught. However, we know that some eventually allow themselves to be found out for lots of reasons, from providing them with fame through to offering them security. I think part of my belief about people with two first names included a small level of secondary gain, as I had always thought it was quite an amusing belief that people found funny and I liked that part of it.

I have to mention that I'm slightly baffled by religious beliefs, not simply because I'm not at all spiritual but due to the conflicting nature of them. Now I'm not wanting to offend anyone here, so if you happen to have a religious belief that's entirely up to you and certainly none of my business. In fact, I confess to being slightly envious, as I'd love to believe in an afterlife, but I simply don't. I believe that when I'm gone, I'm worm food, and that's such a shame as I really and genuinely do want to be thinking that there's more to come for me after this earth. Any belief that someone has that in whatever way serves them well and harms no one else is OK with me, it's when they don't serve them well that I worry. I have an old friend – let's call them James – now James is a good bloke, but he's almost the 'anti-Ken' if you like. He's incredibly negative about everything, always moaning about his lot and believes in just about any or everything spiritual. Many years ago, James went through a rough patch in his life and was seeking answers to some of life's unanswerable questions. In order for him to help himself see into the future so he might know there would be things for him to look forward to, he'd taken to regular visits with a clairvoyant.

One day he came over to see me and, as any good friend would, I asked how his last visit went. He said, "It was brilliant, mate, honestly, she was so good, she knew lots about my life and what's in store for the future." I have to point out that James and I have a very healthy relationship and support each other all the time, however, we have a tendency to tease one another – he calls me a quack and I call him an idiot! So I couldn't pass up an opportunity to let him know my thoughts on what he said about the clairvoyant. After I'd had my say, where I aired my views of caution about what he should and shouldn't believe, he said, "Well, I knew you wouldn't believe me and I spoke to her about you. Once I'd told her about you, she went on to describe you perfectly. She went into a lot of detail about what you look like, the work you do and even how you walk! [By the way, up until this conversation I wasn't even aware I had 'a walk'.] She had a warning for you: she said you need to cut down on eating fat in your diet as it's affecting your health." Now on the whole I have a very good diet and don't go hunting down fatty dishes any more than anyone else and didn't understand what or why his whole clairvoyant experience would have anything to do with me.

We continued this conversation for a while, with him explaining how detailed the clairvoyant had been and how she'd picked out details about him that she couldn't have known. Because of this I thought I'd dig a little deeper and said, "Listen, James, you know the next time you go to see her, can you take your phone in and record what she says to you so I can hear?" I know that was a bit sneaky, but I had my motives. One, if she did say something about me again, I wanted to hear, and that might give me some evidence that there might be such thing as an afterlife and I'd genuinely love that. If it was true, I'd seriously be going to see her myself next week! And two, if, as I suspected, it was all rubbish, then I could tease him about it after. James said, "Yeah, I'm going again next Wednesday, and I don't have to record it on my phone, she charges £20 for a recording!" (Sigh!) So I offered to pay for the recording and gave him the £20. We got together the following week to listen to the recording and before we listened, I said, "Well, was it any good?" He replied, "Absolutely brilliant! She really understands me and gave me some great advice. She even mentioned you again, what you look like, your work and mentioned the fat issue again." I confess I was a little excited to hear what was said, so we played back the recording and listened together.

That was thirty minutes of my life I'm never getting back!

At one point I heard her say, "I can see a man in his fifties, balding!" Guess what? That was it! I know I'm not the only balding man in his fifties. I pointed this out to James and he was in complete denial, saying that I hadn't heard everything and he completely refused to admit his experience was skewed. In psychology we call this 'attentional bias', which I mentioned earlier. This is where you have a bias for things you want to focus on because of your beliefs – more about this later and how it can skew your view of the world, both positively and negatively. Before I finish my bit about clairvoyants, I'm not saying there aren't good ones out there that do good things, it's just my own belief from my own experiences that I've never found one and remember, beliefs aren't real, they're just a thing!

Beliefs can also create habitual behaviour. We've all met the person who's said, "I've always voted Labour and always will!" or, "I've always voted Conservative and always will!" Now I really don't want to get all political on you here as there's enough controversial stuff in the book already. However, politically speaking, the UK's parties over the years have all changed in terms of their policies so much that in many aspects of what they stand for they're so very different from how they were years ago. So what's happening is that beliefs around the values of what something is perceived to represent has created a habit that makes them continually support a political party that was originally created under very different circumstances.

## Chapter Five

# Your Habits

We all live with our own and other people's habits – some are useful and others not so much. I'm not just talking about habits like nail biting or smoking cigarettes, I'm talking about all our habitual behaviour, like driving to work the same route every day or sleeping on the right-hand side of the bed. This habitual behaviour is all around us: we have our favourite mug to drink out of, our preferred route to work and even where we sit in our living rooms in the evening. We continue with habits as they make us comfortable and thinking differently to change them isn't easy.

What actually happens every time we perform the same habit over and over again is that we strengthen physical synapse connections in our brain and the stronger the synapse connections become, the more difficult they are to change. Once our habitual behaviour patterns are established, we often perform them without any conscious thought, turning them into subconscious processes which we may not even notice. Have you ever driven home from work, got out of the car and thought, "I know that journey just happened, but I can't remember all of the steps along the way?" You've managed to drive home in a trance-like state because you've developed your driving home habit to be so strong that your brain has given it little conscious thought. If, during the next time you drive home, you happen to have a little accident because you were experiencing this phenomenon, don't use me as a scapegoat when describing your habit to the police.

Most of our habits are necessary in order for us to function properly. I mean, could you imagine having to take a good look at a chair before asking yourself, "What is that, will it be comfortable, will it break if I sit on it, do I like the colour?" whenever you wanted to sit down. Your brain subconsciously notices all it needs to know to just sit down in the chair, mostly, again, without any conscious thought. This would change, however, if the last chair you sat on broke and you fell to the floor; you'd have particular conscious attention about the next chair you sat on. This breaking chair is an indicator for your consciousness the next time you sit down, ensuring that you pay attention to your behaviour, keeping you safe.

My aim is to help you change in order for you to notice more positive things around you and look for positive outcomes; I need to get you to change your habits and do things differently, which is vital to the success of you benefitting from the book. However, just telling you that isn't enough, because your brain will want you to continue doing the same things you've always done before, so I need to address this issue using a very clever technique known as 'priming'. I want to be able to allow you the freedom about how you think about things and to be able to think of them differently if it benefits you. This involves giving you a signal that you can notice in order to interrupt your subconscious habitual behaviour so that you can give considered conscious thought to situations and alter your behaviour in a more positive way to make people, things and events seem better to you when you find them unpleasant or not useful.

Have you ever made a decision to buy a car, say, for example, a blue VW Beetle? From that point forward, what is it that you see everywhere all over the roads? Yep, blue VW Beetles! Now there aren't any more of these types of car on the road just because you've decided that's what you want. You've just psychologically 'primed' yourself to notice them and they're brought to your consciousness more often; you'll also find that over time you'll begin to notice more and more as you build synapse connections in your brain to look out for them.

It's this priming technique I want to provide for you in this book. At the time of writing this, I had high hopes of being able to provide you with a 'physical primer' and had intended to include a green silicone wristband. Unfortunately, due to the logistics of the publishing process, I've been strongly advised not to, as it might make some retailers uneasy about stocking the book due to the potential of them being lost and the subsequent complaints, etc. I usually give these out at the end of training sessions and people often become very attached to them, saying they feel happier when they're wearing it; it has essentially become a placebo for them.

This 'physical primer' is incredibly powerful, but it doesn't have to be one of my special green wristbands and only has to be something that ensures you notice it. The physical primer is something you can give to yourself, enabling you to notice different things in your world, and I'll explain more about this in a later chapter. If, however, you are super keen to get your hands on one of my coveted green wristbands, there is a way you can do this completely free of charge! Again, I'll tell you about this later (tease!).

Earlier I asked you to change your morning drinking habit or swap the side of the bed you sleep on. I know from experience of asking many people to change these habits that they can feel very difficult to change – there's a reason for this. Our brains wouldn't function properly if we had to make millions of decisions every day about every tiny action we take; for example, should you pick up your morning drink with your right or left hand, or which sock should you put on first. The upside to this is that you can begin to build positive habits that actually help you and assist you in achieving goals you'd like to reach in your life. The key to this is to break old habits, which, in doing so, allow your brain the chance to change thought patterns and provide you a little mental raised flag that says to your consciousness, "I feel different, why do I feel different and why have I done this?"

If you were to swap sides of the bed tonight, I can make one promise to you. In the morning you will physically and psychologically 'get out of bed on the wrong side'. Most people have heard someone say, "What's the matter with you, did you get out of bed on the wrong side?" That's because they've noticed something different about the other persons behaviour; the physical act of swapping which side of the bed you sleep on means you'll be thinking differently in the morning. Noticing that difference in yourself is the stimulus for you to think differently, start breaking unhelpful habits, start building new, more positive, ones and to look out for moments, things and places that make you happier.

Starting new things is always challenging and this is because when we do, we have to focus all of our conscious mind on the new task. If I were to ask you to hop up onto a unicycle (presuming, of course, you're not a seasoned unicycle rider) for the first time, you would find it difficult and have to apply all of your attention to working out the best way to approach the task. After a few days of practise, you'd probably begin riding the unicycle with a lot less thought and after a few weeks riding it would feel natural. Over this time your brain will be building new synapse connections, which become stronger and stronger, making the riding seem much easier. I want you to consider your behaviour when you think of a person, place or task that you dislike for whatever reason, let's say it's someone you're unable to avoid because you have to work with them or, heaven forbid, live with. If it's not possible to avoid them, then you have two options, the first is to continue to feel concerned or uncomfortable about them whenever you have to see them, or the second is to make them seem different so that they don't bother you as much. What normally happens when you see them? Your brain takes you through a habitual process which is difficult to change.

For example, the first part of the habitual process is set off at the very sight of them; almost instantly after seeing them you begin to feel emotional in some way. Then you behave in a particular way that could be to avoid them completely or to talk to them in the same way you always do. At the end of this sequence, after the interaction has ended, you analyse what happened and either hang on to the emotion you experienced because of them or begin to feel better. It's the same sequence every time: a habit! This subconscious sequence comes from the limbic system in the brain, the same part of your brain that is responsible for your fight or flight response and the same part of your brain that takes you towards pleasure and away from pain, so it's important! This is why it's difficult to change the habit because it's the same part of the brain that's trying to keep you alive. It's difficult, but not impossible, to change, and psychotherapists help change these thought processes all the time using subconscious intervention methods. Some of these interventions you could do for yourself if you knew how to do it, which is why I've included the chapter in the book around PEP filters.

In that section, you'll learn how to think differently in order to build positive habits that help you feel better about people, places, things and tasks you don't enjoy. Look, the ironing needs doing so you can put it off for as long as you want, but eventually it's going to have to be done, so you can struggle through it with the hump, or learn to PEP filter it and maybe even begin to look forward to it. Now I promise you what follows is a 100% genuine text message conversation that took place between myself and my partner:

Are you going to the gym tonight darling? xx

This was me asking her if she was going to the gym. As you know, I don't need to go to the gym as I have a perfect body! I'm pretty sure I could give you 1,000 guesses as to her response to this message, but I'm pretty confident you'd wouldn't ever guess the answer. I am aware that some of you might be thinking her reply could contain a sharp comment which asks me why and if I thought she needed to go the gym or something. No! Nothing like that, her reply follows:

Yep!!! In the mood for it.
But gotta re-put my knickers on
first cos I put them on really
wrongly this morning!!!! xx

I told you that you wouldn't guess.

In terms of different people's personalities, I can tell you that mine is one whereby I have a constant internal dialogue with myself which virtually never switches off. I consider things in my head over and over again so often have to reread things to ensure I've understood them properly. Due to the nature of this part of my personality, I had to reread that message a couple of times just to make sure I read it correctly. Also, because of my personality type I found my attention drawn to one particular word: 'really'.

I know it hadn't taken her long to write the word 'really', but she added it all the same. She hadn't just typed 'wrongly', had she? She typed 'really wrongly', so that piqued my interest further. My response to her was this:

LOL. How can you put them on 'really' wrongly???
Did you put both feet in one hole or something? xx

I said this because, in my mind, that was the worst kind of 'really' wrongly I could think of. Also, I'd like to mention that I've shown these slides to literally thousands of people all over the country and of course she knows I use them, she's given me permission.

This particular text message has in the past caused some controversy when I've shown people, and it's not for the reason you might be thinking. It's because I used 'LOL'; who knew it could be so offensive? Did you know there are some words that people use, totally harmless, everyday words, that when used, some people take a serious offence to? A few years ago, I showed this slide at a conference and a lady in the third row from the front suddenly said, at a volume that most people noticed, "LOL, he's used the word LOL, tut tut." She really took offence by my use of 'LOL'. In a moment, I use it again and when I put that slide up, she said in an even louder voice, "Again, he's used LOL, he's supposed to be a professional!" At that point, she folded her arms strongly and looked directly down to the floor, where she remained looking for the rest of my talk. I'd lost her interest because of a word. Now, there's not a lot you can do about this issue with people, because often they don't give you chance to explain their particular aversion to specific words, but I mention it in passing simply so you can be aware of this issue.

So I thought this was the worst kind of 'really wrongly', it turns out I was incorrect and there's something even more wrong. Her reply was:

I've got a leg hole round my waist and the side of my pants is round my crotch! xx

# Brilliant!

There's the second 'LOL.'

It was at this moment that I was struck with a very specific thought. I wonder if you've had the same thought yourself yet?

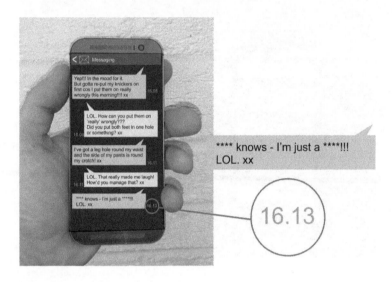

It's almost a quarter past four! She's been like that ALL DAY!

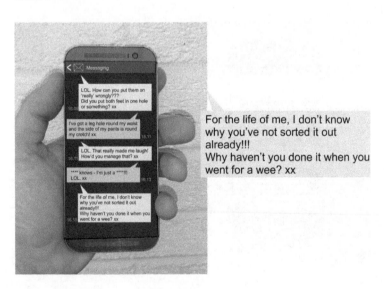

Because I would have done!

Haha. I don't know why I didn't do it when I went either.
I'd have stayed like it all day if I wasn't going to the gym! xx

I know! As I've said, thousands of people have seen these messages now and to date nobody has been able to explain that last message, so feel free to email me if you've an insight that I don't have, LOL.

There is a genuine reason for me including these messages in the book, apart from embarrassing her, and that is to prove a point that while you may never have done what my partner has with your underwear, you've done similar things based upon building habits very quickly. We've all continued to do the same thing we always have done, even though we're uncomfortable. Even when we're not in a good place or are physically hurting, changing a habit is really difficult because of the way our brains have developed fixed thought processes by reinforcing synapse connections in our minds that make it hard to change behaviour.

We've all known people that remain in relationships that make them unhappy, or in a job they really don't enjoy at all, and in some cases, both! They seem to find it almost impossible to make a change in their lives for fear of change itself or the unknown. Psychologically it's easier for them to remain with the status quo rather than pursue potential happiness through change and because of their habitual behaviour they metaphorically keep their pants on really wrongly.

Historically, when I've pitched my training sessions to potential clients, I warn them that, due to the content of my training, there can very occasionally be employees who decide to make changes in their life resulting in them questioning their own current employment. It's obvious to me that anyone who's generally not enjoying their current working position will be far less motivated, not as productive and potentially influence or disrupt other employees to become dissatisfied too. It doesn't happen very often, but every now and then this is a deal-breaker for some of my potential clients who, because of this, decide not to go ahead with the training at all. They'd rather retain the unhappy, disruptive members of their team than make changes to improve their own and everyone else's environment. Thankfully this doesn't happen very often, as I've some very enlightened clients.

# Chapter Six

# Your Senses

The only reason we know anything about the world is because we've experienced it through one or more of our senses. If you couldn't see, hear, taste, smell and touch, would you even be alive? This is actually an age-old philosophical debate that has been considered by many people, and lots of papers have been written around the subject, which consider how you'd even know you were alive if you weren't able to use any of your five senses. With it being agreed in most cases that with the absence of any sensory input at all we'd be unable to learn anything about our environment, then the conclusion to this philosophy is that everything our brain remembers is because of how we've previously seen, heard, tasted, smelt or touched the world.

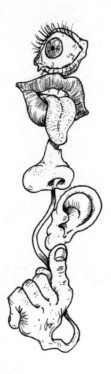

Think of the complexity of an individual's memory. If you and I were standing side by side, watching precisely the same event unfolding in front of us, it would be virtually impossible for us to have an identical memory of the event due to the fact that one of us would have physically better or worse sight, hearing, etc. Therefore, we're going to remember the same event in a different way, with a difference of intensity and a difference of emotional importance based on our previous experience and feelings about events that are similar to the one we've just witnessed together. The reason senses are so important is because it's possible to change the way you experience the world by altering the importance your brain places on the sensory information received from the outside world.

Imagine watching a heartbreak story-type movie with some friends and I'm sure you'll agree that you or some of your friends would begin to feel emotional and get caught up in the storyline. However, you'd also agree that you or some of your friends wouldn't feel particularly emotional about what's going on in the story. How is this possible? I mean, you're seeing and hearing exactly the same thing, at exactly the same time, you're all in exactly the same room and you're all experiencing the entertainment in pretty much exactly the same way. Something has happened with us all as individuals in such that while we're experiencing the exact same thing, we're filtering the same information that's coming into your brains in a different way, and that has affected our interpretation and behavioural response. You may or may not know, or be aware of why some of the things you experience affect you differently to others, it may not even be important to know. What is important, though, is that if you understand this process, you'll realise that it's possible to change your reaction to almost any sensory input received by your brain and automatically alter your emotional response or behaviour. Changing the way you filter experiences by changing the way your brain interprets sights, sounds, tastes, smells and feelings means you can use how you remember the world in sensory format and change how you behave and feel in order to improve your experience of the world.

Later in the book I'll explain how you can use how your brain stores memories in sensory form and how changing these can help you think about future events in a way that allows you the creativity to experience the world differently so that negative people, events, places and things don't have the same impact. Remember the unpleasant person you thought about earlier in the book? Still got the nose, ears and funny voice when you think of them? That's because you changed the way your brain has remembered how the person looked and sounded.

At this point, I'd like to talk a little about what's known as the mind / body connection. It's strange for me nowadays to get to grips with the fact that there remain people in the world that don't understand or even believe that there's an unbreakable connection between our minds and our bodies, and so many people think of the two things as separate entities.

Think about how you feel physically when you watch a TV programme or online video when someone has a *You've Been Framed*-type nasty accident on a bicycle. You watch them fly off, obviously causing themselves a lot of pain and you begin to get an empathetic sense of something unpleasant in your stomach. All you've done is watched a video, but what you've experienced through your senses by watching and hearing the clip has gone into your mind and generated a physical sensation in your body, even though you weren't hurt yourself. I heard a story on the radio recently where a celebrity was talking about their school days, when they mentioned they remembered enthusiastically taking back a piece of marked homework from their teacher and, in the process of doing this, had somehow moved the paper too close to their face and caused themselves to paper cut their eye!

Right now I can imagine the expression on your face as you read that last sentence as the thought of the paper cut causes not just a physical expression to appear on your face but also maybe a reaction in other parts of your body as if you're almost feeling the pain the celebrity must have felt. Lots of people will generate physical sensations in their bodies while watching many different types of emotionally stimulating events, like seeing an animal that's been treated badly or seeing an advert for people who need help due to world disasters.

Also, we've all heard a story similar to the one where a mother is able to lift a car from her trapped baby, and this obviously demonstrates how an emotional condition in our minds can produce extraordinary physical reactions. I've had personal experience of extraordinary mind / body connection phenomena which occurred during a two-hour drive back home after a training session. I occasionally suffer with kidney stones and anyone who's experienced them will tell you the pain can be unbearable. Usually for me it begins with a slight twinge and within just a few short minutes goes from pain level one to ten. Just a few minutes after I left my training session, I noticed the familiar twinge and began to panic a little because I was in the middle of the countryside and miles away from a hospital. Feeling the pain get worse and worse, I was fearful of being in the middle of nowhere with no chance of getting any medical help, so my focus moved to getting as close to home as possible. This focus somehow allowed me to suppress the pain to a manageable level and stop it jumping to a ten very quickly as it normally does. I eventually arrived home and the moment I walked through the front door the pain escalated to ten, and I was taken immediately into hospital for pain relief and treatment.

Sensory information coming into our brains from the outside world can evoke powerful memories that generate emotions which can be positive or negative. Try this exercise and take a moment to put the book down after each statement to really notice what you're thinking about and try to name in your head the emotion the thought has generated.

I'd like you to really take a moment to thoroughly concentrate on each of these next statements and consider them carefully because I want you to recognise that the simple thought of a particular sensory stimulus can generate an emotion inside you.

1. I'd like you to think of a 'smell' that in some way takes you to a memory, that makes you think of a person, place, time, event or thing, that in some way generates an emotion inside of you.

2. Now, I'd like you to think of a taste of something you remember that generates an emotion inside of you, because you're thinking about a person, place, time, event or thing.

3. This time I'd like you to think of a sound, which could be a voice, a song or any other sound that, even if in only in a small way, generates an emotion inside of you because of where it takes you in that memory.

4. Now think of a picture of a person, item, place or event from your, past or present, that generates any kind of emotion.

5. Lastly think of a feeling, it could be warmth, coldness, heartbreak or any other feeling at all that, in some way, produces an emotional response in you, good or bad, because you've thought of a specific person, item, place or event from your memories.

Most people, when doing this exercise, think of things from their past that produce emotional reactions, because they've thought of a loved one, a wonderful holiday, a past family member or a negative event that, quite rightly, makes them feel emotional in some way. However, I wasn't specific about what smell, taste, sound or picture to consider. You did that! The simple act of making a suggestion of you thinking about a sensory input makes you produce either positive or negative emotions; powerful, eh?

What this means is that we can use this cognitive process we all possess to change negative emotions into better ones by changing the way we interpret sensory information in our brains. It's simply a matter of practicing this thought process over and over again in order to build new synapse connections which make us feel better about things we dislike or don't enjoy. We're beginning to install PEP filters that fit in between the sensory information we're receiving from the outside and our hippocampus, the part of our brain that helps us create new neural networks within which basically our memories are stored. In these neural networks our brains neurons communicate with each other through synapse connections which form unique patterns for different aspects of the retained sensory information of our memories. By changing the way we filter our senses we can change the pattern of these synapse connections so that when we recall a memory it delivers back to us different information, changing our emotions.

By the way, if you went through the last exercise and found it difficult to generate an emotion from one or all of those questions, I can help you out right now by reminding you of a sound sensory input that's almost always generated a little emotion in everyone when I've mentioned it to people before, are you ready?

AGADOO!

Our past experiences of sensory input are retained in our long-term memories through the process of developing specific synapse connection patterns and are brought to our consciousness when we notice similar patterns in our present environment again and this affects our emotional responses, habits, preferences and behaviour. All around the world, due to cultural and historical reasons, our personalities develop differently based upon how we experience the world via our senses. For example, in America their favourite chocolate is Hersheys, while in the UK it's Cadburys, and through our sense of taste we're primed to like or dislike these very different flavours. I don't know if you've ever experienced American chocolate, but for me and a lot of other British people I've talked to, it tastes awful, yet millions of Americans love it. The same goes for having bacon with pancakes, I know of a lot of people in the UK that wouldn't think of putting those two things together, but it's a staple in the US and particular flavour combinations based upon what we've experienced in the past affect our habits when it comes to taste.

The same can be said about all of our five senses; what our senses experience with regularity make us accept and often prefer a known stimulant or environment to an unfamiliar one. Take a person that would usually live in an extremely cold climate and put them in a very hot country, and they'd be incredibly uncomfortable and vice versa. The actual temperature in both regions remains either very cold or very hot, but the environment in which we're placed, based upon what our senses are used to, makes us either physically comfortable or uncomfortable when, fundamentally, we're all humans. So the environment, whether positive or negative to us, is simply an interpretation our brains calculate due to what our senses are telling us, which is filtered by the psychology of our previous experiences or memories. What this means is that we already have filters in our minds that allow us to interpret the world through what our senses are telling us, and we can change the way these existing filters work and learn how to experience the world differently.

## Chapter Seven

# Negative Stimulus / Positive Response

A negative stimulus should be thought of as a person, place, event or thing that you experience by initially noticing how they look, sound, feel, taste or smell, which in turn produces an immediate negative emotional response that makes you angry, upset, anxious, nervous, frightened, uncomfortable or any other negative response you'd rather not have. A lot of people believe they're not able to change their negative response into a positive one because their beliefs are so deeply ingrained it has become part of their identity; they can!

Think about a particular task you really don't enjoy doing; it can be anything at all.

**STOP** – REALLY THINK ABOUT A TASK YOU DON'T ENJOY RIGHT NOW!

Take a few moments to really think about something you dislike.

WHAT THING, PERSON, EVENT OR TASK DO YOU REALLY DISLIKE?

They're different for everyone, so it's difficult for me to provide the ideal example for you, but over the years in training people have said things like ironing, driving, cleaning up, cooking, etc. Whatever yours is, think of it for a moment and notice your initial response.

IF YOU WANT THIS BOOK TO MAKE A DIFFERENCE, PUT IT DOWN FOR A SECOND OR TWO AND FIND SOMETHING IN YOUR LIFE THAT REALLY BUGS YOU NOW!

Genuinely stop reading after this sentence and 'THINK' about what your emotional response is; how do you feel when you think about it?

When you have seriously thought about your emotional response and can 'feel' whatever it is you're feeling, read on, BUT NOT BEFORE YOU HAVE REALLY TAKEN A MOMENT TO DO THIS.

I can tell you that for some people their response would be very different to yours and they relish the idea of ironing, cleaning up, driving, cooking and, yes, even to whatever you're thinking about if it's different to these examples. Even now, some of you will be thinking how it could be possible for someone to have a positive response to the thing you dislike. However, the truth is, some people do, and somehow they've altered the way in which their brain filters the idea of the thing to produce a positive response; they've developed PEP filters.

Many years ago, I had a business that went bust and the bills were such that I was unable to maintain the debt. The debt got so bad, in fact, that I had no choice but to take myself down to the court and deliver myself into bankruptcy. During this period I lost *everything*: I lost my home, my business, my car and my wife, and I split up with her having the children, for the most part. It wouldn't be an exaggeration to say it was an intensely stressful and devastating part of my life, which, for those people who've met me that didn't know, would now explain the reason for my receding hairline. This, by the way, is an example of how negative thought processes that generate negative emotions can also affect us physically.

I'm telling you this because I want to explain what happened to me psychologically during this period of time. In the run up to my bankruptcy, I was aware of the mounting bills piling up on my desk and developed some extraordinary physical symptoms. Every time I heard the postman push his letters through my letterbox I instantly felt physically ill, in fact the horrible sensation I was feeling inside was one which I would describe as a feeling of drowning or death. I promise you, I'm not exaggerating. Every single time I heard the letterbox, because I was expecting bills, this awful physical sensation washed all over me and made me physically ill. I now know that this was a severe form of a panic / anxiety attack, where a specific stimulus, not necessarily identifiable, starts a 'mind to body' process that produces these extreme debilitating sensations.

Several months after my bankruptcy, I was finally released by the court, I had a job and was no longer in debt. However, even though I was out of my financial predicament I was still suffering; the door letterbox would go and whoosh – instant drowning / death sensations! I was having to take days off work, which wasn't good as I really needed to stay employed to earn a living. It got so bad in the end that I had no choice but to visit a psychotherapist; can you imagine? The therapist I visited was excellent and taught me lots of things that really helped, but the thing that I think helped the most was a technique he called 'repackaging'. He asked me to think of the process differently and asked what I could imagine coming through the door when the postman arrived that wasn't a bill. He wanted me to think of something nice or positive being delivered rather than bills and all the negative emotions I'd mentally associated with the final demand letters. What he did very well was to ask *me* to think of something *I* thought of as positive rather than him giving me his idea of what he thought would be nice to landing on my doorstep. It would have been wrong of him to suggest something because he had no idea about what would work for me – how could he? He wasn't a mind reader.

So, after a lot of thought, in my mind I turned the thought of a horrible brown envelope with 'Final Demand' written on the front of it into something I've always enjoyed receiving: an Amazon parcel! I chose this because in my mind nothing bad ever comes in an Amazon package, but if it does for you, then I suggest you stop ordering nasty things from Amazon.

Over a few weeks of being creative by imagining different lovely things arriving in my package and practising this thought process repeatedly, I suddenly realised, as I bent down to pick up the mail one morning, that the horrific sensations I'd been experiencing had gone. Can you imagine my relief? They'd gone! It was around this part of my life that I began my interest in psychology, having experienced first-hand the power of psychotherapy. For those that are interested, what happens now when my mail arrives is that I hear the letterbox and get a tiny sensation of excitement, followed by a little bit of disappointment if it's not an Amazon parcel. In the spirit of being nice to each other, which is something I advocate throughout this book, my partner, knowing this about my past and how powerful it's been for me, will occasionally go online and order something small for me from Amazon which is followed by a little text message telling me to listen out for the door. I'm sure you can imagine how much I resemble an excited puppy when this happens. This process of repackaging has essentially turned a negative stimulus – the sound of the letterbox and thought of the bills – into a positive response, so it *can* be done!

So, sensory information is vital for us to interpret the world, and a lot of organisations trying to sell us things already recognise this simple fundamental, so they develop very clever processes designed to trick our brains by the way their message is experienced by us through our senses. They understand how important it is to make things look, sound, feel, taste and smell to us in order to break into new markets or increase the sales of their products or services.

At the time of writing this book, we're in the middle of a massive movement to increase the awareness of the benefits of veganism. I'm not suggesting these people don't truly believe the benefits that a vegan diet would offer us, I'm sure they do. More than this, though, they're aware that converting people to veganism simply by telling us about all of the scientific and dietary reasons why we should give up meat alone will only go so far, and there will always remain an enormous number of people that simply like the taste of meat who are reluctant to change.

With this knowledge, they're spending millions of pounds in development trying to make vegan food taste like meat. They're actually taking cells from real chickens, using plant-based proteins and growing or cultivating them into food that's recognisable by humans as meat. They're getting us to eat plants by making them 'taste' like meat! I mention this because we already trick ourselves on a day-to-day basis when we make decisions about what to eat based upon how the food visually appeals to us. We often select a particular sandwich or other snack because of how it 'looks' rather than how it might taste. Also, at some point in your life you've selected a specific meal based upon how it 'sounds', haven't you? Someone has described a meal they've had to you and your response has probably been, "Oh, that sounds nice!"

This trickery happens all the time in our minds and we can even be seduced into choosing a meal based around our sense of touch, with menus describing their offering as 'comfort food': food based around how it makes us 'feel', our sense of touch! A few years ago, a famous ketchup manufacturer decided to promote a green version of their product that was, to all intents and purposes, meant to taste identical to their traditional red offering. There were lots of reports of the product simply not tasting the same at all, with some people tricking their own brains to think it was different simply because of the difference in colour. This is a great example of how you can trick your brain into experiencing the world differently by manipulating your own thought processes to change the way things are sensed or the way your brain 'filters' the sensory information differently.

## Chapter Eight

# We're All Similar but We're Not the Same

Over and over again I hear people saying, "I always treat people the way I want to be treated!" This statement could be considered to be born from a positive sentiment or at least seem completely harmless. It's my contention that unless you know me very well indeed, you've no idea how I want to be treated! Seriously, how could you possibly know how I want to be treated? I mean, I could be a masochist! I don't want to take away from the sentiment behind the statement but remembering that we're not all the same is really important in order to ensure as many positive relationships as possible with all of the different people we have to deal with.

Let me give you an example. Some time ago I was speaking with someone after a medical conference talk I delivered about this issue and she told me she'd recently had a serious complaint lodged against her at the NHS trust where she worked. She proceeded to tell me that while at work one day, she was taking care of a very vulnerable and sensitive patient who'd been experiencing some trauma in their life. The patient began to break down at one point and was in floods of tears. At this moment the lady reached out and gently held the patient's hand, trying to be as supportive and caring as possible. I'm sure most of us would empathise and realise what the lady was trying to achieve. What actually happened was, when the lady touched the patient's hand, the patient began to scream and was shouting out loud that they were being physically assaulted by the lady. It turns out the patient was dealing with some serious psychological issues brought on by a genuine physical attack that took place several months prior and hence lodged a complaint. I'm sure you can see that her intent was positive, but unfortunately treating the patient in the same way that she'd like to be treated was the wrong strategy in this case. I know this is an extreme example, but I know of lots of people that have issues with physical contact: they don't like to shake hands with people, they don't like other people getting too physically close to them and they definitely aren't prepared to give you a friendly hug if they don't know you extremely well indeed. So the outcome of this is to suggest that rather than treat people the way you want to be treated, a more pragmatic and successful process would be to treat people the way *they* want to be treated.

We've all developed different personalities which have evolved due to the influences we've experienced throughout our lives to date, and if we're to build positive relationships with people that deliver beneficial outcomes for everyone, then we have to change our 'one size fits all' approach to the way we deal with the many different personalities we all come across. If this book is successful, then this may well be the subject of my second, because understanding different personalities and how they interact with one another is incredibly useful in understanding people's behaviour.

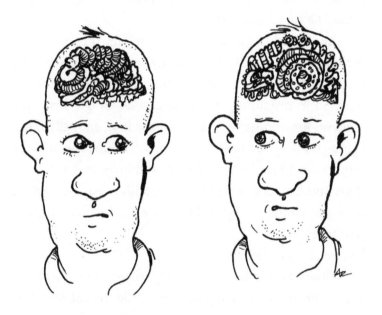

Among these different personalities there are people who behave in ways that we find difficult to understand, simply because if we were in their shoes, we'd have behaved very differently. This doesn't necessarily mean that their behaviour is wrong, it's just different from our own and has developed because of their life's unique set of circumstances.

My partner I and have a great relationship, but this is not because we are the same, in fact we often think very differently. For example, my partner is very happy to cuddle with me and people that are very close to her emotionally, but she really isn't keen on a casual hug from someone she doesn't know very well. This is because part of her personality is on alert more when it comes to her sense of touch. Now for me, I'm not saying there's anything wrong with a good cuddle, but I genuinely believe there should be time limits on them!

This is not because of my conscious thought about 'feeling' the cuddle, it's because my brain is almost always 'on' and I talk to myself about things in my head all of the time. So in my mind I'm thinking, how long's this going to go on for, and surely that cuddle is long enough? But if I stop cuddling her before she stops cuddling me, will she think I don't love her as much as she loves me? Or, if she stops cuddling me before I stop cuddling her, then have I done something wrong and does she not love me as much anymore?

You see, it's a minefield!

While we're on the subject of my partner and differences in personality, I want to give you a little insight into how people can think about the same thing in different ways. If you've read the habits chapter, you'll already have a small insight into my partner's mind and the way she can sometimes phrase certain things.

In order for my partner to drive back home from work, she has to drive around the city's ring road, where a few years ago the council had done some renovation work on a number of houses. My partner and I genuinely do have a great relationship, but by now you'll know that I can be silly and in order to gratify my desire for fun, I occasionally tease her in the gentlest of ways. So here's a conversation we had on her returning home from work one day:

She walked into the lounge and said, "Ken, have you seen the council houses on the ring road? They've all been done up with fresh white walls and those things on the roof."

I replied with, "Yes, I've seen them, they look good, don't they? A great improvement. I'm not sure what you mean about things on the roof, though."

She said, "Yeah, you do, you know, the slanted things, rectangular things on the roof!"

I have to confess at this point I knew exactly what she meant; she was obviously referring to the solar panels the council had installed, but I was in the mood for a little fun, so protested I didn't know what she was talking about.

So I said, "No, I really don't know what you mean, what things on the roof?"

She said, "*Yes*, you do know, you've seen them, you've been by the houses lots yourself, so you know exactly what I'm talking about!"

Still enjoying the conversation, watching her mind work trying the find the words 'solar panels', I said one last time with seriousness, "I genuinely don't know what you mean, do you mean new roof tiles?"

Then, almost as though it came out of the council's installation manual, she came out with this:

"Look, you do know, you're teasing again, they're on the roof, err, you know, erm… Economy… from the sky!"

How wonderful is that?

Human beings are complex creatures with unique personalities that makes us all different in some way; sometimes the eccentricities are difficult to comprehend based on the small glimpse of their lives we experience. Without reading this book, it's pretty unlikely you'd be able to understand my personality with any depth and some of my personality traits would be hard to appreciate unless you understood the bigger picture behind them. If you came to my home, you may be surprised and a little curious as to why there are no light bulbs in the big light located in my living room.

I have a sensitivity to bright lights and find it very uncomfortable going from dark to brightly lit areas. My partner and her kids know about this – in fact I get called a 'gremlin' by them – but for them it isn't as important as they don't have the same sensitivity. For several months after we moved in, they kept popping the big light on whenever they came into the room, which made it particularly unpleasant for me. They weren't doing this to annoy me; they were just in the habit of automatically switching it on whenever they walked in, and we know how powerful habits are. So one day I just removed the bulbs and the next time they walked in their habits began to be challenged, as they reached for the switch and were surprised by the lack of anything happening. They no longer reach for the light switch, which has made it much nicer for me and, to be honest, the only reason I haven't put the bulbs back in is because we've all got used to using the smaller lights, which has now become a habit for all of us.

Taking one small glimpse into someone's life and generating conclusions from the small experience we've gained from the glimpse is called 'naive realism'. Have you ever met someone for the first time and thought, "I don't like you, but I don't quite know why?", or "Oh, there's something about you I like but can't quite place what it is." As an instant subconscious reaction to a person, place or thing, naive realism is a normal, healthy process that allows us to make very quick subconscious decisions regarding our safety; it's part of our fight or flight response to the world.

Naive realism has the unfortunate side effect of causing us to make instant judgements about people, places and things that are often incorrect.

Take a look at the picture below and begin to think of words that you think describe him.

You may or may not have realised that this isn't, in fact, David Beckham, it's a lookalike named Andy Harmer. However, the words you may have thought about – passionate, wealthy, footballer, for example – would still have come to mind. We'll generate attributes about people, things and places based upon our previous experiences, even though they may have no baring at all on the person, thing or place we're experiencing at that very moment. These generated attributes will make us think specific things about them, which in turn generate emotions within us. If you like David Beckham, you'll have looked at the picture and generated positive attributes and positive emotions, but if you don't like him you'll have generated negative attributes and negative emotions, even though the picture isn't actually David Beckham. Seriously, Andy Harmer, the guy in the picture above, might not even be able to play football! We just don't know.

One of the reasons you may even have chosen this book is because of naive realism (in which case, thank heavens for it) based on your previous positive experiences associated with the book's graphics, title or layout. However, I can tell you equally as many people would have passed up on buying the book because of their previous negative experiences associated with the same things.

We need to take great care when generating instant emotions when faced with new people or environments, because naive realism can affect our behaviour based upon subconscious judgements that may not even be real because we're all similar, but not the same.

# Chapter Nine

# Arseh*les

While I believe most people in the world are inherently good and kind, there are influences in some people's lives that, over time, alter their attitude and behaviour towards others that turn them into incredibly selfish, obnoxious, passive-aggressive, bullies, thoroughly unkind, spiteful, abhorrent people, or, for want of a more socially acceptable word that encapsulates all of them (but nonetheless apt), arseh*les! Now I don't want to make excuses for these people, because their behaviour can seriously affect others' emotional states, cause stress and upset, and build anxiety for lots of people around them. However, there are many reasons these people exist and behave the way they do, but I don't believe they're born that way. In fact, as a psychologist, I believe we develop our personality throughout our lives and aren't born with specific personality traits (see 'Nature vs Nurture' chapter later).

Throughout our lives, we all experience the world differently and, as such, learn how to interact with situations and people differently based upon what's happened in our lives to date, what's worked well for us and what hasn't. There are many different types of arseh*les, but their behaviour is similar in that it contradicts our own values and the way in which we'd like to be treated ourselves, or contradicts our own ethical view of the world. It would be true to say that most people are inherently selfish, and while I understand most of us don't want to think of ourselves that way, consider this, why do we look after our own family's care and needs before other families? I mean, we're all human beings, and what makes our family members any more important that other families? I talk about the 'clan effect' in a moment, which could explain this further. All aspects of our personality are on a sliding scale, some people are all-giving and generous to the point that they'll go without themselves in order to help other people. Others simply give to charity just once a year. Some people adore all animals and devote their lives to their well-being, even leaving their inheritance to the local cats' shelter. Others take care of their own pet and shower it, just one animal, with love and attention.

So you can see that when it comes to generosity and the love of animals, these aspects of our personality vary along that sliding scale; the same can be said of arseh*lery. The way we've learnt to behave around others in different situations has enabled us to survive to this point in our life, therefore changing our behaviour is counterintuitive, even if that means behaving badly towards others.

## Fig 1

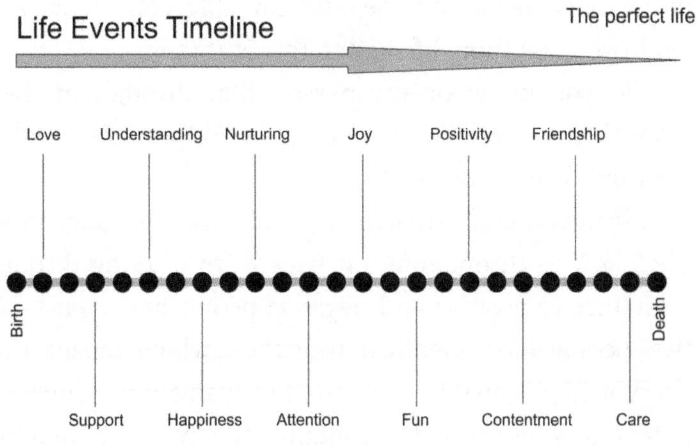

Life Events Timeline

The perfect life

Love  Understanding  Nurturing  Joy  Positivity  Friendship

Birth

Death

Support  Happiness  Attention  Fun  Contentment  Care

# Fig 2

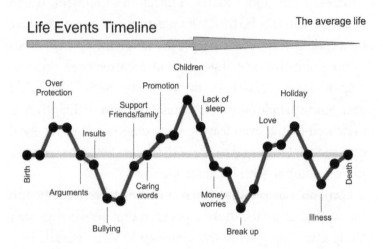

Consider the two images above and think of them as an individual's unique personality DNA. Fig 1 represents a person's timeline throughout their whole life where they've been nurtured positively by everyone at every moment all of the time. In this case, their personality DNA would provide them with a perfectly rounded character with all of the tools they need to be kind, loveable, considerate and resilient to anything life had to throw at them.

Do you know of any person that throughout their whole life has been surrounded by all of these things all of the time? I certainly don't.

It's my contention that most people's timelines look more like Fig 2, as throughout our lives we're working through a mixture of positive and negative people and events. No two people have identical timelines, which means that everyone's personality is different in many ways. Consider a person whose timeline contains mostly events that are below the central line and think about how that might affect that individual's behaviour towards others. As I've said, I'm not trying to defend the arseh*les, but it's easy to see how someone whose timeline has lots of negativity can deliver an outcome which makes their behaviour toward others largely unacceptable. So, when you are faced with having to deal with these unpleasant people, it might help to consider what has happened to them to make them the way they are and, as such, allow you to recognise that their behaviour may not be as a reflection of you personally.

This process takes away the power of their behaviour and offers you the flexibility to place less emphasis on their impact on you. So the next time someone is being an arseh*le, you should take a moment to consider what their timeline might look like. This can take away your instant emotional response which their behaviour would usually invoke and afford you the opportunity to not allow their behaviour to affect you negatively.

If that doesn't work for you, there's a controversial theory in psychology which suggests that *every* behaviour has a positive intention, based on the premise that the statement is true for people with normally functioning neurology and psychology. A large number of people find this difficult to believe and I'm not going to try to convince you it's true. Having said that, I can tell you that if you began to believe the theory, it would help you in lots of difficult situations and, in particular, with the arseh*le. Right now, you react negatively to these people; they make you stressed and cause you anxiety simply because of their behaviour. If you accept that every behaviour has a positive intention, take it on board and make it your life's mantra,

77

the next time someone behaves badly towards you there is now an option for you.

You could become anxious, upset, angry and stressed, or, you could simply ask yourself, "I wonder what their positive intention is?" You may never find out what their positive intention is, but the simple process of just considering that for a moment gives you the chance to halt your own instant emotional response, remain calm and composed in the right frame of mind to deal with them better.

One personal example of this behaviour occurred for me many years ago while I was working for an organisation in London. I was driving into the office very early one morning along the motorway when a fox ran out in front of my two-week-old company car. I made an instant subconscious decision to swerve to avoid the animal. This caused me to hit the central reservation barrier, overcorrect my steering and come off the road down a thirty-foot drop, culminating in me being upside down in a ploughed field. Amazingly, I wasn't seriously hurt but was battered, bruised and cut a little, with the obvious sensations associated with a massive shock. Eventually, I made it to work after calling a colleague to pick me up. When I arrived at work, I was summoned to my boss's office, who proceeded to interview me Gestapo-style. He was genuinely awful about the whole situation and became verbally very aggressive. He didn't believe my story, insisting that I must have had the accident the evening before after drink-driving and he was truly unsympathetic to my accident. Because the car was quite obviously going to be a write-off, his behaviour caused him to react negatively by giving me a final written warning for something that was outside my control.

I'm sure you can imagine how shook up I was after this accident, but to have my boss treat me like this was even more of a surprise which affected me very badly indeed. In normal circumstances, he wasn't a caring boss and most people would have agreed he was an overly strict manager and while I knew about this, I still found his reaction completely unacceptable. The reason I mention this is because we don't always understand the motive behind some people's negative behaviour, which can make it even more difficult for us to accept. Shortly after my accident I decided to leave the organisation because the atmosphere around the office was terrible and his attitude made it difficult for me to remain motivated. Several months after I'd left, staying in contact with some of the colleagues I'd become friends with, I had a telephone conversation with one of them, who told me that in the run up to my accident, my ex-boss had been going through some very serious personal issues, which at least gave me an understanding as to why his behaviour was so abrupt. I have to say that you may not ever be fortunate enough to find out the motives of your own particular arseh*le.

Over the course of my relatively short employment with this organisation, I'd pretty quickly generated a very negative view of this boss and wasn't able to notice anything at all positive about him. The same can happen with people the opposite way around, and we call this 'the halo effect', which happens when we fall in love and notice only the positive attributes a person has, as if seeing them with a halo.

Here's how it works. I mentioned at the start of this book that I'm making the assumption that you have a normally functioning psychology, so if you were to meet me for the first time your normal thought process would be to think, "There's a very handsome man!" – of course it would; after all, you're normal. So if that was your first thought process, your second thought may well be, "Actually, not only is he handsome, he's probably very intelligent as well." Moving on from this, your next thought would be something like, "Not only is he handsome and intelligent, he's very kind too." You might then go on to think, "Wow, he's handsome, intelligent and kind, so I bet he's very loving too." – etc., etc. You get the picture by now; it's a continued process of applying nothing but positive attributes on top of each other until the whole 'halo effect' is complete.

What I'd done with my boss is precisely the opposite and I'd developed a 'negative halo effect' for him, where I noticed every single one of his faults and held him in the lowest esteem possible. Later on, when I found out he was a very caring family man who actually did an awful lot of charity work, I found it almost incredulous and difficult to believe as it went against every aspect of the negative halo I'd built for him. Just take a moment to think about certain politicians you don't like – they may not even be British ones. Do you really think that politician has never done anything good at all in their lives? Of course they have, they must have – even if it was by accident, they've had to have done something good in their lives – but all we notice is the negatives.

I'm pointing this out because we need to take care about this halo effect, as it can stop us from noticing some of the positive actions and behaviours of people once we've dismissed them simply as arseh*les.

Over the years of my delivering training I've often been asked to work with people who are subjected to 'at work' bullying, which is far more common than you might think in various types of work environments. I've met lots of people who've been deeply affected by a bully and they'd developed mental health issues that have gone on to physical health problems. The main problem with bullies at work is exactly that: they're at work, where we can't get away from them and where we have to be to make a living. My aim is to try to help you think about their behaviour differently, because if you have no real option but to deal with the bullies and arseh*les, then you need to find a way to make their behaviour feel different somehow. Of course, if you can do something about it by reporting their behaviour and allowing the processes your employer has in place address the problem, then that's what you should be doing, but if, for whatever reason, you can't escape the arseh*le, then hopefully this section of the book will provide things to help.

It can seem at times that these people are like buses: you can go through periods of life not experiencing any but then three or four arrive at the same time. This may well be true, but it may also be true that when you're going through tough times or living through a time of vulnerability, you're far less resilient to their behaviour and primed to notice them more often.

It's at this moment that I want to make a statement that's incredibly important and even during training sessions where I make a real point of emphasising it, I will still get asked about how to change a difficult person. They even point out that whatever they do in terms of installing PEP filters, the horrible person will still be in their lives and continue to do awful things. So important is this statement that I'm going to write it in capitals:

YOU MAY NEVER BE ABLE TO CHANGE A PERSON'S BEHAVIOUR, BUT YOU CAN CHANGE THE WAY THEY MAKE *YOU* FEEL!

Bad things, horrible people or difficult events may come into your lives, but if you're unable to avoid them you do have an option, which is to change the way you think about them so you don't process the same negativity.

When experiencing bad behaviour from someone else, it's important to try to remain in control of your emotions, which can be difficult, as their actions perfectly connect and oppose your own beliefs and values. Your own beliefs and values are an integral part of your identity, so remaining in control of your emotions when someone represents behaviour that contradicts who you are can be very hard indeed. What I can tell you is that whatever you do and say during an interaction with someone whose behaviour you don't appreciate will be significantly limited if your emotions are running high. Emotional responses caused by these people offer only 'reactive' action from you rather than the far more beneficial 'proactive' actions that could be achieved when emotion is removed from the situation.

Most of the arseh*le's behaviour is repetitive and habitual, meaning they're doing what's worked for them before and behaving in a manner which is easiest for them. If they've behaved negatively in the past and the result of this has delivered a positive outcome for them, then why would they change? Therefore, if you behave in the same way you always do when confronted with the same person's negative behaviour, what's different for them? When you behave the same way you always do with these people, what's actually happening is that you're reinforcing their subconscious thought process, satisfying whatever motive they have behind their actions and delivering a consistent result for them.

So the answer here is to recognise that you're emotional, take yourself away from that emotion in order to remain calm and finally, behave in a different way to the way you would normally. If the arseh*le sees that you're behaving differently, this disrupts their pattern of behaviour, making them realise something has changed, and in order to continue with the interaction, they need to change what *they're* doing.

As an example, I once had a lady ask how she could improve her situation at work where her boss was behaving very badly towards her. Her boss would regularly snap at her, say derogatory things about her work, and make her feel incredibly anxious in the office when he would often approach her desk in an intimidating manner and lean over her.

She told me this was a frequent occurrence and she felt as though she'd have to take time off if it continued because it was making her feel ill. I asked her what she normally did when her boss approached her desk and she said, "I spot him from the other side of the office and notice him marching over towards my desk. As he walks over, I can hear him making comments aloud about whatever I'd done that he wasn't happy with. Then, as he arrives at my desk, he leans right over me and puts some papers on my desk firmly and begins talking too loudly about the issue.

I normally turn away from him so he can't see my face and how what he's saying is upsetting me. I can feel myself becoming very small as I try to move away from him a little; I apologise and tell him I'll try again and that I'm doing my best."

I explained to her what I've just shared with you about changing her behaviour and suggested she needed to do something different, because whatever she was doing wasn't having an impact on her boss's behaviour. Eventually, she took my advice, learnt to think about her emotions and behave differently. She told me later that she'd placed a photograph of herself on her desk that she found supporting, which was from when she was younger and climbed Mount Kilimanjaro. She said the photo gave her the chance to think differently, which removed her negative emotions. Furthermore, she learnt that without that emotion she was able to physically stand up each time her boss approached and stand up straight facing him, which had the effect of him pausing for a moment before talking to her and when he did speak, he was far less aggressive and much less cutting. So this really worked for her; removing her emotions and behaving differently forced her boss to alter his behaviour.

While writing this, I'm reminded to consider that some people don't want to think arseh*les are the way they are because of their experiences but simply want to think of them as, well, arseh*les. The problem here is that their behaviour will still affect you negatively and I don't want that; I want you to have a greater flexibility of thought so that whatever they do doesn't produce negative emotional outcomes for you. Remember, you may never be able to change them, but you can change how their behaviour affects you.

It's also important to explain another possible reason for some people's very negative behaviour. Psychologically we're prone to 'clan-like' behaviour, which means we associate with different groups due to a perceived joint interest. When we're part of a clan, we can often demonstrate fiercely protective behaviour regarding other members. If you think of your family as clan number one, your instinct is to protect your own family above others. However, clans can have significantly more tentative connections than that of our own flesh and blood. If we take a particular follower of a town's football team, you'll understand the clan-like behaviour demonstrated by the team's supporters, who all come together as one all against their opposing team simply because they've chosen to provide their support to a specific team. By the way, they don't necessarily have to live in the town whose team they support; it's simply their support that provides them admission to the clan. So a clan can be a group of people who work together who all have some similarity, whether it be a significant similarity or a tiny one. You'll notice that occasionally at work that people who work in the same department can form clans and can operate defending their department's actions over others, even though they're working for the same company. This is why some organisations encourage team building training, so they can bring people together across the organisation to encourage them to realise they're actually all in the same clan.

So, it may be that the person that's behaving badly towards you may simply not have found a connection with you where they're able to subconsciously include you in their clan and this can make their behaviour very defensive. The good news is these clans are changeable, so it may be a matter of finding common ground from which to begin a subconscious basis for a clan they'll allow you into. If a football supporter's home team isn't playing, they'll move on to support a local team over one that's in another region. If their regional team's not playing, they'll go on to support their country's team over another country's team and so on.

When considering people's bad behaviour, you should also think about the fact that some people can be arseh*les by accident. Somehow they touch on our own sensitive subjects that they don't actually know even affect us. I can assure you that there will definitely have been times that I've done this without knowing when I'm sure other people placed me in this category. One instance I can remember from my youth was a day when I was having a chat with my dad about the new £1 note (yes, a new £1 note, not coin), that was due to be released into circulation that day. I mentioned earlier that my dad was a veteran of the Second World War and suffered PTSD due to his experiences. One side effect of his PTSD was stuttering, and it was something he was embarrassed about, but until the day of £1 the note's release, I wasn't aware of his embarrassment, I'd just taken it as part of who he was.

It may sound silly, but as a youngster I was kind of excited to see the new note and because my mum and dad owned a corner shop, I was expecting to see one at any moment. While eating lunch with the family, I told my dad I hadn't seen the new note yet and asked him if he'd got one, and he told me he hadn't. My brother Michael was due home at any moment and his employer at the time paid him in cash, and as my dad knew this, the conversation went something like this:

Me: "If you've not got one and there aren't any in the shop, when do you think I'll be able to see one, Dad?"

My dad: "Don't worry, Ken, your brother will be home soon and I'm sure M-m-m-m-mick will have one."

Me: "Well, I guess I'll just have to wait for 'M-m-m-m-mick' to get home then, won't I?"

My dad: *WHACK!*

Now I'm not advocating his smacking, but I instantly realised I'd been an arseh*le. However, I'd done it entirely unintentionally because I wasn't aware of his emotion behind his stutter.

As I said, I can't condone his behaviour, but PTSD is an incredibly serious affliction which can deliver a variety of extreme symptoms that cause the sufferer to behave in ways that they seem to have very little control over. It's easy to understand when you take a moment to consider the extremes the person has been through. I don't believe we provide sufferers with enough support even today, so I know my dad would have had little or no support at all after the Second World War.

One last thing to consider when dealing with difficult people is the use of 'emotional coinage'. Anyone who's ever studied the subject of 'negotiating skills' will know about the term 'coinage' and how it can be used. Fundamentally, coinage is used as a bargaining tool where one party offers something of little or no value to them, but is of much larger value to the other. When considering emotional coinage, it's important to point out that some people think of different emotions with different emphasis. What this means is that someone's negative behaviour towards you may be because they're not placing the same value on certain emotions as you. They may believe they're providing you with a large degree of emotional support, when in reality they're offering you something you might perceive as coinage. Of course, this can happen the other way around and there may be things you can do to provide emotional coinage to them, which makes an enormously important difference to them. You'll need to consider how each of your emotions might be being valued differently and remember we're all similar, but we're not the same.

If, like me, you've experienced a large number of arseh*les throughout your life, I'm quite sure you'll understand the enormous level of restraint I've demonstrated in this section by not taking this incredible opportunity to name some of them. It wasn't easy! While naming them would have been entirely unprofessional and I genuinely wouldn't want that, I'm hoping that parts of this chapter will help you recognise people like this from the descriptions I've provided in order to help you deal with them better.

## Chapter Ten

# Changing Your Existing Filters into PEP Filters

PEP filters allow you to think more positively about negative things; they provide self-empowerment, allowing you to behave in a way you'd prefer in negative environments and offer you the opportunity to perform better in those difficult situations. Everything you've experienced in your life to date has subconsciously built your existing psychological filters through which you define your world – some work well for you and others don't. In order to improve your experience of people, places and events, you'll need to improve the existing filters you currently have and turn them into PEP filters. The techniques I'm about to explain will enable you, over time, to have an immediately improved response to events that would previously have resulted in negative responses, but you'll need to practise them several times in order to build different synapse connections. The practise of these mental techniques will change your existing filters into PEP filters and build new habitual behaviour that provide better instant emotional responses.

In psychology there's a term known as 'the plasticity of memory', which refers to the ways in which our memories change over time or with influence. This plasticity means our memories can be changed in different ways that deliver different cognitive processes when the memories are recalled. It's this plasticity that PEP filtering takes advantage of in order to change your own memories so that when they're recalled, they produce more beneficial cognitive processes that improve your emotional response.

Here's how it works.

In order to really focus on this process, you're going to have to really think about each of the steps. Some people find it easier to close their eyes while they're doing it, or at least take themselves somewhere quiet where they can go through the process without outside interference and where they're not disturbed.

You know that everything you experience comes into your brain because one or more of your senses has experienced it, then the sensory information is processed by how your brain remembers similar events in the past and delivers an appropriate response, or behaviour from you, based on your usual habitual behaviour. Think of phobias, for example. If you suffer from a phobia, you'll know what happens, how awful it can feel to you and how your response is irrationally emotional. There are lots of people with arachnophobia (the fear of spiders), which is irrational in the UK, as virtually all of the spiders you'll come across in day-to-day life are harmless to humans.

By the way, most phobias are developed when we're younger and it's easy to see how. If you imagine the tiny 'you', knee high to one of your parents, for example. There you are, playing or watching the TV or something, and then this God of a person that looks after you and does everything for you walks into the room. Your small child brain, that isn't even physically fully formed, makes you look up at your parent's face to see the look of pure horror that they're demonstrating. You then hear them shout, "*Spider!*" and your attention is taken to the little black crawling thing as you watch them point to it and they then behave in a manner that you're not used to, which lets you know beyond all doubt that they're experiencing pure fear. At that very moment, what do you think your little brain interprets from this response? Of course, you are bound to think, if that person that's everything to me – my provider and carer – responds like that when they see a spider, then I'd better take note of that because it must be important. If that's not enough to make you afraid of spiders from that point forwards, the fact that they behave this way *every* time they see a spider by looking frightened to death and shouting, "*Spider!*", then the reinforcement of this will teach you that it's not just important, it's vital. So the behaviour is learnt in a very powerful way that means you begin to behave in the same way and build the habit of a phobia.

So the stimulus is you using your sight to notice the spider and then your brain remembers instantly how you habitually behave and takes you from zero to terror almost instantly.

PEP filtering is a concept whereby you use a technique that places something in your brain in between the part of the process that 'sees' the spider and the part that remembers your normal habitual behaviour. This can be done for anything, any negative stimulus at all. It can be the person you have to deal with but don't like, the job or task you have to do but don't enjoy, or any instant emotional response you'd rather change, like road rage / supermarket trolley rage, for example.

PEP filters are created by adjusting the way you think about any specific negative thought process by changing the way your brain recalls how it's stored the sensory aspects of the memory. This is done by you changing what I'm calling 'subsections of senses', or SOS.

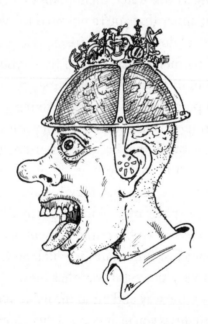

SOS are how we specifically remember each part of each of our five senses. Essentially, it's a breakdown of the detail of how we've remembered each of our sensory experiences of particular events. When you 'see' something, for example, you're producing a picture of that thing in your mind and it's the detail in the picture that we need to look into to work out exactly how you've remembered what you saw. This detail in your memory of what you saw is what I'm calling the SOS of 'sight'.

So let's take you through the process of exactly how you build your own. There's a diagram on the following pages where you should write down the details of your SOS for this exercise.

Begin *now* to think about a specific thing, person, and event or task that you don't enjoy and firstly start to think about how you remember that issue in terms of sight.

When you think about how you 'see' this issue in your mind, ask and answer these questions:

Do you see the memory as a colour or black-and-white picture?

Do you see it as a still photograph or as a moving picture?

Do you see it as bright or dull?

Do you see it as close or far away?

Do you see this thing as though you're looking through your eyes or can you see your face?

Each of these is an example of SOS for your sense of sight.

Now let's move on to your sense of hearing and ask and answer the following questions:

What can you 'hear' when you remember this issue?

Is the sound loud or quiet?

Is the sound muffled or clear?

Is the sound high- or low-pitched?

Is the tempo of the sound quick or slow?

Each of these things is an example of SOS for your sense of sound.

OK, having answered these questions about how you remember your issue so far, move on to how you feel physically and emotionally when you remember your issue:

What are you 'feeling' when you think about your issue?

Do you feel relaxed or tense?

Do you feel hot or cold?

Do you feel comfortable or uncomfortable?

Does it feel hard or soft?

Does it feel rough or smooth?

Each of these is an example of SOS for your sense of touch.

I imagine by now you know where I'm going with this, so let's move on to taste:

What, if anything, can you 'taste' when you think about your issue?

Is it pleasant or unpleasant?

Is it sour or sweet?

Is it salty or bland?

Is it hot or mild?

Is it smoky or rich?

Each of these is an example of SOS for your sense of taste.

So, finally, move on to how you remember your issue in terms of how it smelt.

What, if anything, can you 'smell' when you think about your issue?

Is the smell weak or pungent?

Is it a smell you like or dislike?

Is it floral or plain?

Is it chemical or fresh?

Is it earthy or musty?

Each of these is an example of SOS for your sense of smell.

I can't emphasise enough how *important* it is to take your time and remember as much as possible and to go through every sense and really try to notice anything you can. In some cases, you might struggle to find something for every sense – that's OK, but *really* try!

Once you've gone through the process of identifying how your brain has remembered your unpleasant issue in terms of specific SOS detail, I now want you to try changing the memory in your mind by asking yourself after each change whether the memory feels better or worse.

Obviously I can't guide you here, because everyone remembers things in very different ways and there are numerous combinations of SOS for every individual memory. The positive aspect of this, though, is that it's unique to you and therefore *you* will be the best judge of what seems better with every change you make.

So what I want you to do is go through the previous list, changing the SOS of your memory and noticing positive differences; something like this:

If you think of your issue and see it in black-and-white, then change it to colour and ask yourself if it seems better. Make it brighter if it's dull and do the same thing. Turn it into a moving picture if it's still or vice versa and notice how that seems.

Go through each of the senses, changing every SOS you can think of as you go and notice how it seems better when you settle on each one that makes the memory in some way improved. For example, think about what you remember hearing – was it loud? If so, make it quiet and notice how it seems to you then. If it's hot, then change it to cool and notice how it seems then. If it tastes sour, then change it to sweet and notice how it seems different. If it smells musty, then change it to smell fresh and notice how that seems different. These are all examples of how you *might* change the SOS, but you should be considering at every point what aspect of each sensory memory you could change that would make it seem better for you and change it to *whatever* you need to make it seem better to you.

After you've done this, you should now consider any positive changes you could make in terms of how you remember your negative issue and change it. For example, when you 'see' your memory, how does your face look in the picture? It's likely you won't look particularly happy when you see your face because you're thinking of something negative. So what I'd like to do is ask you to think about exactly what you'd prefer to notice about the expression on your face – that lets you know you're emotionally how you'd prefer to feel when you're in that environment. Would you like to see on your face that you're relaxed, happy, concentrating or professional? Whatever you'd like to see on your face or indeed add to that picture that in any way lets you know it seems better is the result you're after!

Then move on to sound. What sounds could you add or take away from the memory that make it seem better? So keep the good sounds and lose the bad ones.

# STEP ONE

## Your Issue
Specific thing / person / place or task

| SIGHT | SOUND | TOUCH | TASTE | SMELL |
|-------|-------|-------|-------|-------|
| Think about how it looks. | Think about how it sounds. | Think about how it feels. | Think about how it tastes. | Think about how it smells. |
| Change it until it seems better. | Change it until it seems better. | Change it until it seems better. | Change it until it seems better. | Change it until it seems better. |
| Colour to B&W Brighter or duller Closer or further Still or moving Notice how your face looks in the picture and change it so you look how you'd prefer. | Loud or quiet Muffled or clear High or low pitch Fast or slow tempo. | Tense or relaxed Hot or cold Comfortable or uncomfortable Hard or soft Rough or smooth | Pleasant or unpleasant Sour or sweet Salty or bland Hot or mild Smoky / rich | Pleasant or unpleasant Weak or pungent Floral or plain Chemical or fresh Earthy / musty |

# STEP TWO

Your Issue with
IMPROVED
sensory details

Now add beneficial detail and
remove anything negative

| SIGHT | SOUND | TOUCH | TASTE | SMELL |
|---|---|---|---|---|
| What could you add to what you're seeing to make your issue seem better? | What could you add to what you're hearing to make your issue seem better? | What could you add to what you're feeling to make your issue seem better? | What could you add to what you're tasting to make your issue seem better? | What could you add to what you're smelling to make your issue seem better? |
| What could you remove from what you're seeing to make your issue seem better? | What could you remove from what you're hearing to make your issue seem better? | What could you remove from what you're feeling to make your issue seem better? | What could you remove from what you're tasting to make your issue seem better? | What could you remove from what you're smelling to make your issue seem better? |
| This can be anything at all, realistic or not. | This can be anything at all, realistic or not. | This can be anything at all, realistic or not. | This can be anything at all, realistic or not. | This can be anything at all, realistic or not. |

# STEP THREE

## PLAY

As if you're watching a movie from start to finish:
run through your issue SEVERAL times,
ensuring you notice all the improved sights,
sounds, feelings, tastes and smells.
Add anything positive
and remove anything negative.

## PAUSE

Pause your issue at the end and notice that it's
better because of all the detail you've changed.

## REWIND

Now rewind your issue from where you
paused at double speed!
Finally add a really silly song or sound.

## REPEAT

Repeat the whole process SEVERAL times, run
the movie normal speed, pause and rewind in
double time with the silly song or sound.

Now take yourself through the process of changing, altering, omitting or adding how the memory feels, tastes and smells, removing anything unpleasant and adding things that make the memory seem better. You can add or change *anything*, it doesn't even have to be realistic, it just has to make you notice that the memory seems better.

Once you've made all the changes you need and begun to notice how it's beginning to seem better for you, you'll then need to watch the whole memory from start to finish, including all the positive changes, as if you're watching a movie. This process will need repeating several times, in fact as many times as possible, until you begin to notice that you've removed some of the negative emotion from the memory.

Then I want you to see the whole process coming to an end, as if you've paused the movie, with you successfully getting through your memory achieving everything you'd wanted – seeing, hearing, feeling, tasting and smelling all of the things you'd prefer that makes the whole thing seem better and more positive.

The key to the success of installing these PEP filters is you repeating the process several times. The number of times you'll need to do this varies for everyone, dependent upon the strength, importance and nature of the memory.

Finally I want to add an element of silliness in order to diminish the seriousness of the memory, so once you've practised running through the new changed memory several times and paused your memory right at the end, I want you to rewind the whole memory as if you've pressed the rewind button on your remote control and literally see yourself moving backwards to the beginning of the memory at *double speed*. As you do this, I want you to add one last thing. As your memory runs backwards at double quick time, add the silliest song or sounds you can think of. Take a moment to think of a song or sound that you find personally silly.

That's the whole process! You'll need to run through the whole thing from start to end at normal speed, pause, then rewind at double quick speed, hearing the silly song or sound. Again, repeat this process several times until the thought of the memory seems better. The process of repetition is really important as it strengthens synapse connections of the transformed memory in your brain and alters pre-formed synapse patterns. Think about why companies replay their advertisements over and over again on TV. It's so the adverts become ingrained in our memories, creating a psychological primer for the next time you think about specific purchases and it's obvious that repeating adverts works for them; they're expensive, so if showing an advert just once was powerful enough, they wouldn't continue to pay for more.

Also, next time you're watching the TV advertisements, notice how you're bombarded with sensory information about how their clothes make you 'look' better because you're wearing their designs. They'll also describe to you about how you'll 'feel' better because of their medicines or because you're sitting on their furniture. Even more than this, they'll go to great lengths to tell you how much more attractive you'll be because of the 'smell' of their perfumes / aftershaves and how their food's 'taste' is not just food, while doing all of this you'll also 'hear' music and sounds meant to generate emotions. Over the last few years, some brands have even introduced their own sound jingle to reinforce our memory of them with not just pictures but catchy sounds too. If it were possible to include ways to support their brands with the use of touch, taste and smell, you can bet your life they would; roll on smellyvision!

The next time you have to experience your issue again, or indeed any experience that might in a small way be similar to your issue, you'll be reminded of all the changes you've made and the experience should seem much better to you.

PEP filter successfully installed!

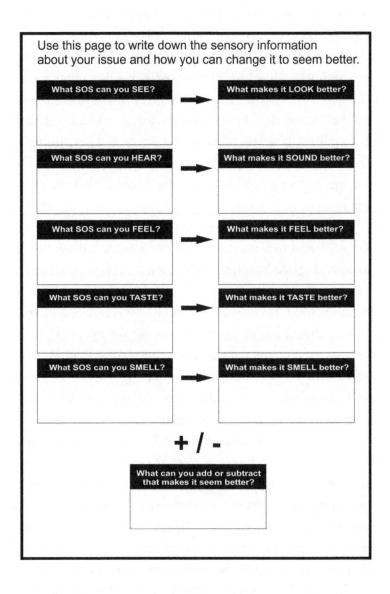

Use this page to write down the sensory information about your issue and how you can change it to seem better.

| What SOS can you SEE? | What makes it LOOK better? |
| What SOS can you HEAR? | What makes it SOUND better? |
| What SOS can you FEEL? | What makes it FEEL better? |
| What SOS can you TASTE? | What makes it TASTE better? |
| What SOS can you SMELL? | What makes it SMELL better? |

**+ / -**

What can you add or subtract that makes it seem better?

I don't want to influence you with my own use of SOS changes, but I've noticed during training sessions that if I invite a volunteer to the front of the room and guide them along this process so everyone can see how someone else changes their SOS, then people not only understand the process better but also always see a positive outcome to the whole thing from the volunteer. As it's not possible to do this in a book, I'll explain about an issue I had and how I used PEP filtering to help. Please remember, though, that this is *my* example and the SOS changes were right for me, but you need to make the changes that are right for *you*.

During the early part of me starting Tarragon Training, I was invited to a meeting with the head of a department at an NHS trust hospital to discuss a training opportunity. During the meeting, the department head said he'd recently been experiencing a higher level of complaints from patients about his staff than would normally have been expected. The nature of the complaints seemed to be about how the staff were communicating with the patients and a lot of misunderstanding was taking place that was, in turn, generating the extra complaints.

The department head asked if I could deliver training to around 200 of his staff over the course of about ten sessions working with approximately twenty people attending each session. He suggested the sessions should contain information about better communication and improved bedside manner. I told him I'd be happy to do this and we set up some convenient dates in our diaries. At the end of the meeting, the department head said this: "Thanks for agreeing to do this, Ken, but I need to mention a couple of things before you start this training. I have to tell you that there are a good number of the people you'll be training that can be difficult and I've a lot of stubborn people in my team. Also, most of them have had different communication training previously and they believe they're already good communicators. So is there any way you can deliver these sessions with a different title other than one that contains the word 'communication'?" I told him I'd have a think about that and our meeting was completed.

I'd like to point out that the training sessions were to take place at one of the hospitals own training rooms, which was located in a particularly old part of the hospital. The training room itself was ancient; it looked like it hadn't been painted since the place was first built and was known for always being too hot. If this was not bad enough, it was located in a part of the hospital almost next to the STD clinic, and in order to get to the room I would have to follow signs from the outside of the hospital that directed people to the STD clinic, so people could make their own conclusions as to the purpose of my visit every time they watched me enter.

It came to the day of the first session and I walked uncomfortably to the room. It wasn't just the clinic signs that were making me a little uncomfortable, it was also the fact that in deciding how to deliver this training I'd ignored the department head's advice. I'd overconfidently thought I was good enough to get away with it and thought my style of training would be entertaining enough for me to call the session 'Communication and Psychology', and the attendees had already been informed about the title – oops!

So there I was, already feeling a little uncomfortable; I walked into the roasting hot, deeply depressing training room and noticed the twenty heads that turned to look at the person audacious enough to train them on communication, all of which had incredibly stern looks on their faces. I spent the next part of the day delivering my session to one of the most belligerent groups of people I'd trained so far. I mean, they were awful! They were argumentative, defensive and purposely unreceptive, even to the light-hearted sections I'd included in order to keep them engaged. There were raised voices from some of them complaining that they'd been asked to go on the training at all and as I left the session, I felt as though I should probably rethink my career choices. The day came when it was time for the second session and I'm sure you can imagine my trepidation, but I wasn't feeling as bad as I could have, because the day before I'd spoken at a conference for a different organisation where I'd received rapturous applause at the end of my talk and been fed salmon for lunch, so I had a renewed confidence in my abilities. Unfortunately the word had gotten out to the next group about the nature of the first session. I wouldn't have thought it possible, but if anything the second group was worse than the first, the room was even hotter and I could have sworn I noticed people talking about me as I followed the signs to the STD clinic.

I left the session feeling dejected, and when I got home, I had a conversation with my partner about it, telling her I didn't know why I was even doing this gig at all as the people were so awful, and that I knew I'd be worrying a little all the time up until my next session with them. She said, "Hold on a minute, aren't you the person who trains people how to think about things differently so they seem better? Why don't you just put what you train into practice yourself and change it?" She was obviously having a day when her knickers were on correctly, because she was obviously right again.

I didn't have to go back and do the rest of the training but came to the realisation that all of my audiences weren't always going to be as receptive as the one that provided me with a salmon lunch and knew that I needed to do something about it for the future anyway. I applied my own PEP filter for these situations and here's exactly what I did.

I thought about what I saw when I concentrated on the issue; here's a list of my memory in terms of sight, including all of the SOS I could think of associated with sight:

> Concerning clinic signs.
> People talking about me.
> Awful, dull room decoration.
> Agitated, unhappy faces of people in the room.

Then I thought about what I heard in my memory of this event and the sounds I was hearing, noticing all of the SOS I could think of associated with sound:

> People whispering about my visit to the clinic.
> Angry, loud voices coming from everyone in the room that came after the silence when I entered.
> The high-pitched sound of the heating system in the room.

Moving on to what I was physically feeling, I was remembering and noticing all of the SOS I could think of associated with touch:

- » The room was swelteringly hot.
- » I was feeling sweaty.
- » I was also feeling anxious about their reaction.

My mouth was also dry, so I was feeling that too.

In remembering what I was tasting, in this situation I couldn't place anything specific in this particular memory. It's often the case, by the way, that you may not be able to recall a memory for every sense, because it may not be particularly relevant to every issue. Had my issue included a memory where I'd been eating or drinking something, I'd have thought about it, but this one didn't.

Finally I thought about my issue in terms of smell, remembered what I could smell and noticed all of the SOS I could think of associated with smell:

- » There was a musty smell from the old room.
- » I could also smell the usual good old hospital smell that lots of people find unpleasant.

So there's the detail for me of my specific issue, and I remind you again that these are my own individual sensory aspects of my specific issue and unless they're exactly appropriate to your own, you shouldn't use them but notice exactly what *you* remember.

To install my PEP filter, I needed to change the SOS in order to make it seem better.

Focussing initially on my visual sensory memory:

» I recognised that I wasn't seeing my own face in this memory, so I changed it so that I could and asked myself how I'd like to be looking that would make the issue seem better, so noticed I looked calm and professional.

» I swapped the clinic signs to say 'Excellent Tarragon Training'.

» I saw the people talking, but now they weren't talking about me going to the clinic.

» I changed the dark, poorly decorated room into having a brighter, more modern appearance.

» I swapped the agitated look on people's faces to be smiles of enjoyment.

I then moved on to what I was hearing in my memory:

» I changed the loud, argumentative people into people chatting quietly about good things they'd heard about my training.

» Rather than angry voices, I heard positive chat and laughter.

» I removed and ignored the sound of the heating.

In this particular memory of my issue, what I was feeling seemed more important than my other senses, so I spent a little more time changing these:

» I turned the room into a cool, breezy space and began to actually notice how my body would feel if there were a light fresh breeze.
» I changed the sweaty feeling into me feeling dry and comfortable.
» I noticed my breathing, slowed it down and swapped the anxiety for a relaxed sensation.
» I'd taken with me a bottle of water to refresh my mouth so it was no longer dry, which, by the way, I genuinely do in real life now for all my sessions, as it has been known to offer people genuinely positive benefits when they're nervous, as in stressful situations our mouths often become dry.

While in this memory I wasn't really tasting anything, but I asked myself what I would like to taste to make the issue seem better. For me, the thought of something minty seemed to make me feel better, so I added a minty flavour to my memory.

When it came to my sensory memory of smell:

» I swapped the musty and hospital room smells to a smell of fresh laundry, which to me is always pleasant.

Lastly, I considered what else I could remove from or add to the memory that would make it seem better:

> » I immediately thought that having one of my old respected lecturers in the audience who was nodding with approval seemed to help, so he was added.

Then I ran through the whole process as if it were a movie from start to finish, thinking of the memory like this:

I saw the 'Excellent Tarragon Training' signs and noticed the calmness on my face in the bright, modern room with people smiling. I could hear positive chat and nice things being said, followed by laughter. I spotted my old lecturer enjoying the session. I felt the breezy room, calm, relaxed, cool and comfortable. Then I noticed the smell of fresh laundry and a minty taste.

In order for me to begin to notice that the memory seemed better to me, I reran this process seven or eight times and on the last time I paused it right at the end, noticing that it felt better and was seeing how well the whole training session had gone. The last part of the process is to run it backwards at double speed, actually watching myself moving backward and for me, the silliest sound I could think of was the theme tune to *The Benny Hill Show* (showing my age there). I have to say that seeing myself going backwards in this situation while playing the *Benny Hill* tune in my head physically made me laugh out loud.

I then ran through the whole process from start to finish as if watching my movie, pausing each time at the end and rewinding with the *Benny Hill* tune and found that after doing this seven or eight times (or for you, as many as necessary until you notice your issue is improved in your mind), I began to feel very different and genuinely much happier about the whole issue. I'd installed my PEP filter!

What I can tell you is that prior to doing this I'd thought I was going to be worrying about my next training session all the time prior to me delivering it. I honestly didn't! In fact, whenever I did think about it, I genuinely smiled a little.

So, on the day of my next session at the hospital I was honestly feeling very different about it and something very strange happened. As I went through each part of the experience in reality from start to finish, every time I'd have previously noticed something negative, I was reminded of the positive SOS I'd changed it to. In fact, the next session went so very much better and I genuinely did notice people enjoying it, with me enjoying it much more too.

I then came to a realisation when I thought about the groups I'd worked with before; they genuinely weren't as bad as I'd thought, I'd been focussing so much of my attention on the negativity that I wasn't even noticing the positive responses. Of course, parts of the session were still challenging and some people still weren't happy about having to receive this training, but on the whole the sessions were a success and of course those people watching me head towards the STD clinic weren't talking about me at all.

***

# Anna's Story

In writing this book, I've mentioned many times how important it is for you to work with issues in a way that suits you, rather than changing them in a way that I personally would find helpful to me. I've given you an example of how I changed a thought process to make it seem better to me, but the changes I made won't necessarily be the right ones for you. So, I asked my partner, Anna, to contribute to the book to provide you with another example of how *she* used PEP filters to improve one of her memories, so she could feel and behave differently when she came across similar experiences in the future. The rest of this section, apart from my interjection, is written by her and in her words:

*Ken asked me to write about an issue that bothered me and to use his PEP filtering process to explain how it helped me. One issue I have is with a manager I had at a previous job because of the way she made me feel and how it affected me. I instantly thought of this particular woman when I started reading this book, as the thought of her still bothers me when I remember her. The problem at the time was that I needed the job and couldn't see a quick way out, so I had no choice but to put up with her every day. Virtually every day she'd make me feel stupid, silly, belittled, like shit and made me feel like crying. I'm actually feeling a little bit emotional right now as I remember my situation. One day she asked me to get her a sandwich during worktime and I felt really annoyed with her using me like that when she'd been treating me so badly. On the way back to work, I was so pissed off I dropped her sandwich on the street several times. She deserved it; she was a cow.*

Ken back again for a little interjection. I just want to point out that during training sessions when I've spoken about bullying at work there have been a number of people who've expressed that they wanted to get revenge for the way they've been treated. I want to say that the thought of 'sandwich revenge', or any other type of revenge, may very well seem like a good idea and a lot of people will hold on to this feeling for many years. I can tell you, though, that from a psychological perspective, revenge is motivated by an 'away from' origin (more about this later) and while you may feel there are just desserts occurring with revenge, it means that you take the moral low ground and it goes against the positive psychology message I'm trying to get across with this book. It may provide an instant gratification, but it can deliver significant negative consequences for you, which in the long run can affect your own positive psychology. Revenge, in turn, can go some way to turn you into an arseh*le as you learn negative behaviour. So I'm not an advocate for revenge in 'sandwich' or any form.

*So I went through Ken's PEP filtering process, following the instruction about what sensory information I noticed when I remembered the issue and here's what I thought.*

*Sight: I was looking through my eyes in this memory but if I change it so that I see the memory as though I could also see my face, I can see me looking scared and worried. I could also see her fringe, greasy face, her very greasy hair and her dull, drab clothes. I could also see a window behind her and I remember a dark green plant on top of the filing cabinet. I also saw her on one side of the desk with me on the other.*

*Sounds: The only sounds I can remember are the sound of trains going by and us talking with her saying things like, "You've not done this right, you've done it all wrong!" in her whingey voice.*

*Feelings: I was feeling defensive, struck numb, forgetful, emotional, not good enough and self-conscious. I shrunk! The whole thing made me feel, urrgh!*

*Taste: I can't remember any specific tastes but do remember having a dry mouth.*

*Smell: At first I found it hard to remember any smells but, remembering what Ken had said about taking time to really try to get some detail in as many of the sensory memories as possible, I started to remember her smelling unclean or musty.*

*Those were all the things I remembered about this issue. So I changed the SOS to make them seem better to me and here's what I did.*

*Sight: I changed her drab clothes into bright, cheerful ones. I changed her face so she now looked kind, was smiling and had clean hair. I didn't change the plant or the window because I saw them as insignificant and they just didn't bother me. I changed my scared / worried face into an expression that made me look calm.*

*Sound: I changed her whingey, annoying accent into a Lancashire accent, as my nana had such a lovely accent from living in the Blackpool area. Every time I hear that accent I'm filled with such a lovely sensation. I didn't change the train sounds because I grew up living next to a train track and I guess the sound of them reminds me of home.*

*Feelings: I had previously felt that I was numb, self-*

*conscious and had shrunk, so I changed this to me feeling happy, relaxed, normal-sized and confident.*

*Taste: I couldn't really remember tasting anything, just having a dry mouth, but the thought of a lovely, hot cup of tea made this sense feel better. So I added that!*

*Smell: I changed the musty and unclean smell by putting some lovely flowers in the room. They smelt gorgeous!*

*Adding / removing things: In thinking about what I could add or remove, I thought about removing the desk between us and seeing us sitting next to each other on the same side of the desk, and that seemed to make the memory better.*

*After I made these changes, I went through the process of watching the whole thing, like a movie, from beginning to end, five or six times, noticing how much better my memory seemed.*

*Running through my movie, I saw her bright, cheerful clothes and her smiling face with clean hair, with me looking relaxed, calm and smiling. I saw us sitting next to each other without the desk between us. I heard her talking in the lovely Lancashire accent I like so much with the nice sound of the trains in the background. I noticed how relaxed I was feeling and that I felt confident. I began to taste the lovely hot cup of tea and smell the lovely fresh flowers.*

*On the last time I ran through my movie, I paused it at the end, rewinding it at double speed to the sound of the* Birdie Song *playing.*

*Finally, I went through the whole thing five more times, running the movie forwards, pausing it and then running it backwards at double speed while hearing the* Birdie Song.

*That was the whole process done.*

*I actually can't believe how easy this was and how much*

*it has worked towards improving my memory of this, as I can honestly say that I won't be able to think of this woman, or anyone who reminds me of her again, without smiling. I seriously can't believe I just said that! Can I just say that I wasn't sure about being included in this section of the book, but I'm glad I am, because being included actually made me go through the PEP filter process and it's made a difference! I want to apply PEP filters to lots of other things now.*

✳✳✳

Lastly, I understand how difficult finding your own SOS in order to create your own PEP filters can often be and it can prove to be tricky. So if you find the process tough, I'd like to suggest you take a few moments when you're alone to consider things you remember that have physically made you feel good. Take yourself back into your memory and begin to allow yourself physically to feel the positive emotional sensations. Once you've practised this several times, you'll begin to recognise that you can indeed build positive emotions from thinking about personally satisfying memories, and these sensations, including the process you go through to generate them, can be applied as positive SOS during the PEP filtering process.

# Chapter Eleven

# Visualisation

## (How You See the World)

There have been many books written for a variety of purposes solely around the subject of visualisation, because it has historically proven to provide consistent results for lots of people. I want to talk about it here a little, though, because the visual aspect of the previous chapter is so important to the process of allowing you to benefit from positive results. Types of visualisation are used in lots of psychotherapy disciplines in order for people to provide their own mental view of seeing themselves in improved situations. Virtually every top sportsperson these days uses the services of a sports psychologist in order to improve their performance and all of them at some point would have used techniques associated with visualisation.

Sportspeople will spend several hours – both away from the physical practise of their sport and also during their games – thinking about themselves performing well and never seeing themselves performing badly. A golfer, for example, might begin by taking themselves through the process of thinking about a particular hole on a course as if seeing it from a drone flying over from tee to green. They'll notice every hazard, the hole's particular shape and level, while considering the best possible approach to the green in the smallest number of shots. They'll then visually see themselves standing at the tee and notice how they're standing and looking in a way that lets them know they look exactly how they need to begin to make a perfect shot. After this they'll see the ball and notice the position of their club in relation to it, then they'll see every aspect of their shot from noticing their backswing to following through and hitting the ball. Finally they'll see themselves hitting the ball perfectly and watching the flight of the ball, with it eventually ending up in the hole *every* time, never considering it missing. This is often called 'forward projection', where people see themselves doing something successfully in the future that they haven't yet achieved.

Boxers will do similar things with visualisation while considering their sport. They'll notice how they look fit and strong as the walk into the ring (even doing this while sitting at home and not physically practising their sport) and notice how all of their punches are landing precisely how they'd like. They'll notice in their minds that they are dodging the punches from their opponent, with them looking frustrated not being as effective as they are. Then, finally noticing themselves victorious at the end of the fight holding up the winner's belt. Running athletes do the same thing, noticing things from exactly what it is they need to see in order for them to know they're pacing a race correctly and how physically fit they are, through to running over the finish line in first place.

This visualisation essentially builds and strengthens synapse connections in the brain, which exercises their mental practise and thus teaching them repetitively, precisely what they need to do to perform at their very best in actual practise.

These techniques should not be left to benefit only top sportspeople, though, because they can be very beneficial to everyone in everyday life. Thinking about how we could perform well during a presentation you have to do at work, for example, can provide you with much greater preparation and enable you to practise it to perfection in your head, noticing how people are enjoying what you're saying and seeing yourself calm, relaxed or whatever you personally would like to look like to notice how well it's going.

You may have a difficult meeting or awkward discussion you have to go through in the future, so visualising this with all the positive attributes attached will help you mentally practise a positive outcome, which makes it far more likely that in reality at the time of the meeting, you'll actually perform in a way that works well for you.

When practising visualisation for anything at all, you should remember to notice whatever it is that makes you see yourself, however you'd like, that lets you know you're doing whatever it is that reminds you that you're performing precisely in a way that benefits you. For example, I might tell you to notice how relaxed you look in a particular situation, but in actual fact you'd prefer to look serious or professional, so my suggestion wouldn't help. You need to see what's right for you! Also, I would suggest you keep your visualisations to yourself and don't tell people what you're visualising. This is because some people might want to impose their own views, which make you question how you're seeing a particular situation that might help them but doesn't help you. I've used visualisation in the process of completing this book and regularly see myself receiving copies of my finished manuscript and posting what I know will be a very happy photograph of me holding my book on Twitter. If you're reading this, then that picture will already have been posted, so go check it out and see my visualisation in reality.

Having said how powerful visualisation is and how beneficial it can be, remember you're using just one of your five senses in this process, so imagine how powerful PEP filters can be when you use all five of your senses!

## Chapter Twelve

# Attentional Bias and Motivation

Officially, the term attentional bias in psychology refers to the degree of attention we allocate due to the level of threat we're faced with; however, I'm hijacking the term for the purposes of explaining how much our attention is biased based on any stimuli that's important to our individual beliefs.

The last part of the 'Changing Your Existing Filters into PEP Filters chapter explains how my attention was biased towards specific negative aspects of my experience when training groups of people at the hospital. There are lots of people that do this in different situations for different reasons and I mentioned attentional bias before in 'The Importance of Silliness' section.

Think about a party environment where you're with a group of people, chatting and engaging with them. You then turn around to walk away to get a drink or go to the loo, and a moment or two after you've moved away from the group they all start laughing loudly. Some people at this moment will automatically begin to think the group are laughing about them. The odds are they've simply stumbled across something that has nothing to do with you but made them all laugh. If that describes you, then all you're doing is letting your attention become biased towards what you *think* they might be laughing at based upon your beliefs – and we know beliefs aren't real, they're just a thing.

Sometimes people can find themselves in life going through a series of negative events and begin to feel as though the world is conspiring against them. It's often also the case that a lot of the good things in their life are still there, but their attention is biased towards the negative events, as though there's nothing positive around them. How many people do you know that are like this? I don't need to tell you how serious this is and how this sort of bias can lead to severe depression. Of course, I'm not trying to say these events aren't serious to the individual – they are and can't be ignored. What I'm saying is that if you focus too much of your day-to-day thinking on all the negativity while disregarding the positivity, then this can become an issue.

Earlier on in the book I talked about superstitions. Attentional bias could be another reason these superstitions are supported by those that hold them. Imagine a deeply superstitious person who, one day, prior to going out of the house to work, had to put their umbrella up inside, accidentally breaking a mirror, and on their journey spotted a black cat while only just noticing they'd walked under a ladder and not had anything wooden around to touch when telling themselves that everything would be OK. Actually, even when writing that and knowing that I'm not superstitious, I realise I've written a series of events so potentially influential to some people's behaviour that even I'm a little uncomfortable with it. That's the power of these beliefs!

But really, wouldn't you agree that the person in this scenario would spend pretty much every second of the day looking out for something negative to happen? Of course they would, their attention would now be so seriously biased towards noticing just about everything that is in any way negative, that they'd be bound to notice something bad at some point, which then goes to support their belief further.

Attentional bias can work both ways, of course, and it can be a conscious decision you make to ensure you're noticing all of the positive things around you that actually make you feel good rather than the other way around. Over time this bias becomes part of your 'go-to' thought process and in fact the more you do let your attention be biased in either way, the more this can affect your overall view of the world. You're actually creating and building new synapse connections in your brain that make you think about and notice more of the things that make you happy and placing much less emphasis on the impact of negative experiences.

Understanding your own motivation behind the reason you do certain things will help you modify your own attentional bias. Motivation is a complex subject, which I talk about in detail during training for management teams in order for them to deal with the varying enthusiasm they and their teams have for different aspects of their jobs. Delivering a detailed understanding on the subject of motivation is not the main aim of this book, but I do need to explain a few principles so that you can motivate yourself to actually put some of the techniques I explain into practice and this involves doing something different. While I'm discussing motivation, I'd like you to not just think about how these principles work with you, but also why they're important for people you have to deal with.

In order for someone to be motivated to do something, they require autonomy, mastery and purpose.

Autonomy is important, because while some people need to be led, they also want to feel a degree of self-satisfaction so they can notice their own achievements. The knowledge that we've achieved something autonomously is self-empowering, which is why the chapter on PEP filters encourages you to do this yourself and simply guides you through the process. Once you've done it correctly yourself, you'll be more motivated to do it again.

Mastery provides the opportunity to notice self-improvement, because most of us want to believe we're moving forward in life and getting wiser or more skilled in some way. The more you practise building PEP filters, the better you'll become at working with them successfully, hence you'll be more motivated to use them more often.

Purpose is vital in motivating yourself or other people, because as humans we need to know why we're doing something and in fact the word 'because' has been studied in scientific experiments, whereby simply adding the word 'because' to a question significantly increases compliance with the question's recipient. In one particular study of the word 'because', they tested people around their response to them being asked if a person could use the photocopier before they did.

With the question, "May I use the copy machine before you, please?", it resulted in sixty per cent of the test subjects agreeing. The question was then changed to, "May I use the copy machine before you, please, *because* I have to make some copies?" Even with the addition of the quite obvious last part of that question, this resulted in an incredible ninety-three per cent of people agreeing to allow the other person to use the machine first. Lastly, the question was asked including the word 'because' together with what seemed to be a good reason why: "May I use the copy machine before you, please, *because* I have an important deadline?" This only resulted in a tiny increase, with ninety-four per cent of the people complying. I think this demonstrates the power of 'because' and that providing a purpose, no matter how important, motivates people to act. In this book I've provided you with lots of reasons to use the techniques and a purpose for the whole process.

As I said a moment ago, think about how your interactions with other people satisfy these three necessary principles for their motivation.

You're also far more likely to have your own personal goals realised if you're motivated 'towards' the end goal rather than 'away from' something you don't want.

For example, are you reading this book because you want to be happier and notice more positive things (towards) or because you don't want to be a misery (away from)? The answer may be a little of both, but you're far more likely to be motivated to actually do the things I've suggested if your motivation is 'towards' rather than 'away from'.

So for you to get the most from this book, you should let your attention be biased towards the positive outcomes and become motivated to make the changes you need, taking you towards the positive benefits it could provide. If you haven't done this so far, you've probably put the book down and given up on it anyway, so there!

# Chapter Thirteen

# Nature vs Nurture

As I've said, the process of how to install PEP filters can be difficult to understand, but hopefully you've successfully found the best way to apply and alter the different SOS in a way that works for you. On occasion, I've worked with people who've told me they don't believe it's a 'natural' process for them, but I believe it's a matter of practise because we know whenever anyone practises something or repeats the same psychological process over and over again, they'll eventually become proficient. This would suggest they 'nurture' themselves in order to realise their eventual potential with most tasks.

The whole 'nature vs nurture' subject is a minefield and can be argued from lots of different perspectives.

However, because of my knowledge around psychology and experience of how psychotherapy can alter people's perspectives, I believe as personalities we're born equal and it is only the way in which we're nurtured with positive and negative influences throughout our lives which forms them.

I don't believe we're born with the personality we end up with as if we're pre-programmed by our genes to behave the way we do today. I do believe that our genes affect our physiology but also that we're not predetermined to experience every positive or negative attribute that lies within our individual genetic blueprint.

At this point I want to say that I am aware that this is an incredibly controversial subject and has been argued with as much passion from different points of view as religion. I support the view that nurture has much more impact on our personalities than our genetic nature. I support this belief because I have very personal experience and examples of this that have been proven lots of times due to my own lineage. However, if your beliefs support an opposing view, then let's say *vive la difference*; feel free to skip this chapter and move on to the next where I'll be less controversial.

There was an amazing story in the news some time ago, which was followed with a TV documentary, where three male triplets were separated at birth and had found each other by accident in their adulthood. The documentary went on to discuss how similar the triplets were – not just physically very similar in appearance but also in their behaviour and preferences. The documentary went on to demonstrate several similarities the triplets had which could, on the face of it, go some way to disprove my beliefs about nurture, but I had a different view on this.

Firstly, the whole aspect of finding similarities between them went towards making this a much more entertaining programme, without which would still have made the story good, but not amazing. Secondly, I think you'd agree that if you'd been one of these triplets, wouldn't you be far more fascinated by your similarities with the other two than your differences? Over and over again, the documentary demonstrated the handful of similarities in preferences the triplets shared and didn't discuss the thousands of other examples where they were very different indeed, so I would put this down to their desire to continue to support their own personal beliefs and values due to attentional bias.

Additionally, I think there are lots of, but not all, people who I feel would rather relinquish personal responsibility for their personality and behaviour because it's easier to tell themselves and others it's not their fault but the way they were born. More often than not, in my experience, when people do this, it's when they're focussing more on the perceived negative aspects of their behaviour or personality than on the positive ones. They'll tell you that they've been successful at something because of all their hard work and dedication but not attribute their success to their hereditary genetics.

Let me try to offer a couple of examples that support my argument for nurture over nature. We know that women whose mothers suffered with breast cancer are statistically more likely to also suffer with the same condition. Statistically this is correct, however, not *every* woman whose mother had breast cancer will necessarily get it themselves. If we were simply a product of our genetic blueprint provided to us by our parents, then how can this be? There's something else at play in these situations, something that means our physical health isn't necessarily predetermined by our genetics. I'm not going to say I have the answers for the biological or genetic reasons but would ask you to consider environmental factors. We know that we learn behaviour from our parents, so wouldn't it be easy to extrapolate that the child would likely learn similar lifestyle choices which could have a negative effect on their health? If the parent made poor lifestyle choices or was subjected to a great deal of stress, wouldn't the child learn from this and notice similarities between them? Additionally, with the knowledge that you're more likely to suffer from hereditary disorders, couldn't this act as a massive nocebo, making you more likely to concern yourself and have this affect your psychology? We also know that stress causes significant health issues, which means that because of what we're experiencing from the outside world through our senses, which is then interpreted by our brains, we experience negative health consequences.

Therefore, from this point you could begin to consider what the effects of negativity might have on your health, and you know that people react differently to the same outside stimulus. Some people become stressed due to a specific environmental factor and some others, experiencing the same environmental factor, don't. If we take this whole thing through to what I think is a logical conclusion, it could be argued that we may have the ability to switch on or off both negative and positive aspects of our genetic DNA based around how we interpret the world and how our brains process the information.

If we look at neuron cells, we know that they require protein in order for them to produce the necessary sodium for our brain's synapse connections to function correctly. Proteins are made up of amino acids which interact with each other, and this correct interaction allows the protein to fold in a specific 3D structure. If the amino acids don't interact correctly, then the protein will fold in a different way, which then causes the brain to produce incorrect signals that affect us physically, leading to unwanted physical effects.

Amino acids are affected by heat and cold – their environment – which means the proteins fold incorrectly and deliver undesirable reactions.

So, I want you to think about a 'cell' for a moment and consider the consequences of its correct function based upon environmental influences. Of course there are physical environmental factors that affect the performance of cells, such as drinking alcohol, smoking or excessive heat, etc. However, there are other environment influences that affect cells and these are how we process information through our senses. You know how it feels physically when something very negative occurs in your world – you can have a horrible experience and feel physically awful. The way in which you've thought about an issue has delivered physical consequences for your body. So, changing the way you think about different aspects of your life more positively produces the opposite effect, making you feel physically good. Experiencing positive events in your life makes your cells work well and delivers positive physical sensations for you. Turning negative thought processes into positive ones using PEP filters could actually deliver much more than simply making you think differently; it could actually make you feel physically better too.

When I talk about the subject of nature vs nurture, I'm often asked about specific examples where people want answers to situations that they believe contradict my bias towards nurture. I've been asked on many occasions about families that have twins where someone might say something like, "Well, I have twins and have treated them identically and they've turned out with very different personalities, so how can that be?"

In reality, of course, it's impossible for two twins to grow up being treated by their parents in an identical manner. What happens when one twin baby starts to cry but the other doesn't? Wouldn't you be more likely to pick up and comfort the crying baby and leave the other in the crib? Now I'm aware that as babies we have limited cognitive functions, but we are primed with basic emotions and you shouldn't think for a second that the baby left in the crib hasn't noticed you've picked up the other and are comforting that one while leaving him / her laying there. These small differences add up and take us away from the central line of personality illustrated in the timeline diagram in the 'Arseh*les' chapter.

Additionally, while you think you may well be treating the twins identically, then what about other environmental factors they experience, from one being closer to the radiator and being warmer, or what other people say and do with the twins differently, either in your presence or in your absence. It's impossible to provide two people with exactly the same life experiences, even with your best intentions in place, and all of these small differences, over the years, add up to enormous personality variances.

One more thought about cells: if we know that cells are affected by environmental factors, then what do you think you are physically? That's right, you're on very basic terms, just one enormous bunch of cells constructed in a 'you'-type shape!

Now before I finish this chapter, leaving you thinking that I don't believe that nature plays any part at all in your psychological development, I genuinely do, but not in any way as much as how you've been nurtured. There are some aspects of emotional response we seem to be born with on a very basic level. For example, new-born babies will still be affected by some sensory stimuli without any obvious previous learning; they'll flinch at bright lights and react to loud noises even though they've no idea what the stimulus means to them.

Also we know that new-born chicks will automatically react to the sight of a bird of prey even though they may never have seen one before. There are some theories that believe there may be a reason for this. These theories suggest that if, during your life, you recognise through emotional reaction that something is vitally important to your survival, the importance of this message is somehow transferred genetically down to our offspring. So, my beliefs and thoughts about the effect of nurture and personality development shouldn't be thought of as the whole answer but rather an insight into things you can change, rather than things you can't.

## Chapter Fourteen

# Happiness

Most people are inherently selfish, with very few people being truly altruistic. I'm not saying there aren't people out there that do lots for charity and truly feel they're doing lots for other people; there are. There are many different types of altruism and there have been lots of psychology papers written around the subject which discuss the cause or motive behind them. So while most of us feel the compulsion of nepotistic altruism and look after our immediate family members, the causes for moralistic altruism vary. Helping people that seem to deserve our help feels good, so while the consequences of helping others benefits them, it also makes us feel good too. Ultimately, if you have a normally functioning psychology, as a human being virtually everything you do is to strive towards your own happiness. We do this in very different ways which depend upon our previous experience, personalities, available resources and individual motives. I mentioned earlier that there are some people who seem to wallow in their own misery and actually claim to be happy being miserable; that seems like an oxymoron, right? The essence here is that they *are* happy and have built habits which support their belief that they are in fact miserable. Again, as I mentioned earlier, breaking or changing these habits isn't easy and can be very uncomfortable which, during the process of change, make us feel unhappy. Therefore, remaining miserable is easier for some people than going through the difficult act of change.

I'm not claiming to be the authority on happiness, for that I'd recommend you look to the many wonderful authors on this subject like Dr. Andy Cope. What I am saying is that with the knowledge that most people feel better when they're happy than when they're miserable, applying the PEP filter technique to as many of the negative things, people, places and events in your life as possible will help make these unpleasant things seem better, making you happier!

# Chapter Fifteen

# Psychological Priming and Your 'Physical Primer'

Earlier, in the chapter on habits, I wrote about a 'physical primer' and how powerful it can be. The green wristbands I usually give out at training sessions are tools that are used as a visual stimulus for people that wear them. I'd love to be able to say that my green wristbands contain special powers, but unfortunately, they don't! *Any* new thing you decide to adopt wearing, that you wear for a specific purpose, primes you to remember why you're wearing it in the first place.

What you need to do is find your own physical primer. This can be almost anything at all but 'needs' to be something you don't normally wear. It can be a new or old watch, a bracelet that you don't usually wear, a noticeable ring or any charity wristband (which I highly recommend, as you'll not only be helping charity – an act of kindness – but also be helping yourself too). Whatever it is you decide to choose as your physical primer (it doesn't have to be expensive), put it on now!

Every time you notice your physical primer is an opportunity for you to stop behaving the same way your habits would usually make you behave and prime you to notice things around you that you'd prefer to notice, and consider if you're behaving in the most positive way for you. If you haven't put it on yet then do it soon, because the sooner you do, the quicker you'll begin to notice new, nicer and more positive things in your world. These things can be anything at all, but your personality will have a particular preference for whatever these things are. The important thing here is for you to think about what things *you'd* like to notice: it could be things in nature, more smiling faces, beautiful buildings or even animals that make you feel happier. If you're not bothered about sunsets, then it would be remiss of me to tell you to make sure you notice more of them, simply because they're something that I appreciate. So, take a few moments to answer these questions and make a note of them here:

1.  What things in life do I like that make me feel happy, could I notice more of?

    _____

    _____

    _____

    _____

2. What activities do I want to start doing, or do more of?

_____

_____

_____

_____

3. Whenever I notice my physical primer, I want to remember which positive things about me?

_____

_____

_____

_____

4. What habits would I like to start, stop or alter that would make me feel better?

_____

_____

_____

_____

5. What personal goals would I like to achieve?

_____

_____

_____

_____

Now, because of the plasticity of your memory that I talked about earlier, every time you notice your physical primer, you'll be reminded of the things you wrote here.

I want you to keep your physical primer on for approximately six weeks. The reason for this is that six weeks is about the right amount of time for you to begin to notice differences in the way you're thinking and to start to make positive changes in your life that begin to build your positive psychology and start becoming more resilient to negative influences.

Wearing your physical primer is like having a tiny version of me on your shoulder (but in this case, wherever you're wearing it) reminding you to rethink during those times you begin to focus on negative outcomes rather than positive ones and give you a chance to notice how you're thinking and ask yourself, "Is this really how I'd like to think or is there a better way?" It's there to tell you to continue to visualise and forward project towards the things you want in life, while also reminding you to install PEP filters for those things you find unpleasant or uncomfortable.

I'd like to strongly suggest that whatever you wrote / write in the previous section you keep entirely to yourself. Whatever you wrote / write was purely for your own benefit and there's a strange psychological phenomenon which occurs when you actually announce things you're planning to do or change, whereby the very act of telling someone makes it more difficult to actually achieve what you want. There are lots of judgey people out there (I know the word is judgemental, but I prefer judgey) who can easily make the things you're planning feel irrelevant or stupid. This is primarily because seeing other people improve can make some people feel as though they're being left behind in some way and at that moment they don't have the same heightened motivation to entertain their own improvement. If, after a short period of time, you begin to forget you're wearing your physical primer, which can happen, move it to somewhere else on your body – swap wrists if it's a watch or charity wristband, or swap fingers if you chose a ring and you'll start noticing it all over again.

I know from people telling me after training sessions that they use their wristband as a stimulus to remind them to behave in lots of different ways and some people become very attached to them. At the beginning of this book I told you that writing doesn't come easy for me; this is mostly because my internal dialogue is always 'on' and the thoughts in my head run much faster than my fingers can type. Writing is a motivational challenge to me and there have been several times during the process of writing that I've felt like popping on the TV rather than focussing on the chapters, or found my thoughts wandering into whose email I should be replying to rather than finish a particular paragraph.

I don't know if you remember Mr Motivator from some years ago? He was a guy that used to perform aerobic exercises on morning television and used to get very enthusiastic about trying to get us all up off the sofa and exercise along with him. I've used my green wristband personally as a physical primer when writing this book; it's my own personal little Mr Motivator, reminding me how important it is to get the book finished during those times my mind was wandering. It's also a reminder to visualise the finished article and picture the happy expressions on people's faces as they're reading it. I'd also visualise people benefitting from the book, seeing them feeling better about difficult situations and emailing me with nice words saying how much they enjoyed it. I know there will be people who don't appreciate this book – that's obvious, I can't appeal to everyone equally – but in the same way that I don't look at the miseries when I'm delivering talks, I'm not visualising the ones that don't enjoy this book either. So, if you're reading this, then I guess my own physical primer worked for me, as the book is finished and at this moment there's little point in me worrying about those people who haven't enjoyed it. I can't change it now!

Earlier in the book I gave you a little tease about how you could get your hands on one of my green wristbands for free. As I've said, there's nothing magical about them at all, but I am aware that some people will still want one, maybe to get the full *PEP Talk* experience. So, here's how you get one for free:

Follow me on Twitter, take a photo of you wearing your own physical primer and send that to me with a tweet explaining how well it's worked for you. After that, I'll private message you to get the address (UK only) where you'd like me to send it and I'll pop one in the post for you absolutely free of charge! Barring any unforeseen events, of course. @tarragonken

# Summary

Hopefully you've understood the influence habits and beliefs can have on positive behaviour.

I want this book to be a catalyst for the positive change(s) you'd like to make so that these changes make you feel more empowered to behave in ways that help you perform in areas of your life that make you happier. The key word there, though, was catalyst, because simply reading this book won't change anything, but the action you take by employing the techniques included in it can! Because of the nature of my work, I am, more than most, aware that it's this action on your part that's the most difficult thing for me to ensure happens which is one of the reasons I've included the 'Psychological Priming and Your Physical Primer' chapter. Your physical primer is a reminder for you to notice those times when you're behaving or thinking in ways that don't serve you well and to take action.

Obviously this book contains some very personal examples of how I've dealt with different aspects of adversity, from my 'mother' story through to my bankruptcy. It also contains examples of how your brain has the capability to alter physical pain and affect your emotional responses. I'm not claiming this as something that's going to change the world, but the contents have the capability of providing you with tools to make significant improvements to aspects of your life, which I've seen the result of after observing other people go through the process.

Hopefully you've learnt how beliefs and values can sometimes be a limiting factor in producing more preferential behaviour, and that habits, while difficult to break, can be changed to provide you with beneficial results. I also hope I've given you an insight into possible reasons to consider why some people seem to behave badly and in doing that, helped you to begin to understand there may be ways you can think differently so that they don't affect you so negatively in the future.

You should have taken from this book that it's probably not a good thing for your psychological well-being to allow all the negative aspects of some things to continue to affect your emotions and that noticing more of the positive things that generate nicer sensations for you is far better for your own psychology.

I hope this book turned out to be the PEP talk for you

I'd intended it to be and that it helps you take action to move towards more of the things in life you'd like.

So, keep wearing the physical primer, dump unhelpful habits, build all the PEP filters you need for any issue you might have and say more nice things about yourself to yourself more often. The benefits are valuable and once you've noticed some of them, you won't want to go back!

*You* are in control of your life and you do have the ability yourself to move towards the things that make you happier, you just need to take action and remember, this could be your last chance to disco!

Many thanks.

# Acknowledgements

As I said at the start of this book, writing it didn't come easily to me as it felt like a very daunting task. Along the way I've had a lot of people help and support in different ways so I wouldn't want to miss this opportunity to thank you.

To Harvey and Mimi (my children) for your continued belief and moral support.

To Joshua Maton for his knowledge of biology and helping me explain the science.

To Helen Stubbs and Inga Vann for being my willing guinea pigs and wonderful advice.

To ADzArt for providing some amazing illustrations!

To Dr. Andy Cope for your wise words, advice and wonderful recommendation.

To Eddie 'The Eagle' Edwards (such a lovely guy) for reading PEP Talk and providing an amazing quote.

To my publisher, The Book Guild, for recognising the books' potential and putting up with my constant questions.

Finally, but most importantly to Anna, my wonderful partner. Without your totally selfless support this book wouldn't have been written. The book would also be much shorter without all the content I've been able to talk about, including your knickers! With love. xx

# Contact

Ken Hancott can be contacted by getting in touch with Tarragon Training via the website or Twitter.

www.tarragontraining.co.uk

@tarragonken

ken.hancott@tarragontraining.co.uk